For use in the Home, Business Colleges and Schools of Grade : : : : : *Edited and Published by* ZILLER OF KANSAS CITY Copyrighted Seventh Edition 1938 Eighth Edition 2001 2008	# F. W. TAMBLYN'S # HOME INSTRUCTOR ## IN # *PENMANSHIP* *A complete and concise instructor in penmanship for teachers and pupils everywhere who desire to acquire a good handwriting, to gather inspiration and to learn more of the truths concerning this subject.* Containing complete information as to position, movement, and writing materials, etc., with practical illustrated lessons in Plain Business Writing, Artistic Writing, Flourishing, Lettering, Drawing, with a large collection of original gems of Pen Work. : : : :

A special thanks from the publishers is extended to

Jan Powell
for her keen editorial eye aiding us in presenting these works
and to

Dr. Joseph Vitolo
for his cooperation in coordinating the historical events and
his enthusiastic advocacy promoting the appreciation of penwork as a skilled art form
and lastly to

Stephen A. Ziller
for having stayed the course over a masterly 59 year career.

8th Edition, 2nd printing
Copyright © 2001 - 2008

Published by:
Ziller of Kansas City
12310 Wenonga Lane, Leawood, Kansas, 66209 U.S.A.
Phone 913-648-6374 --- FAX 913-648-6399
Email: richm@zillerofkc.com --- Website: www.zillerofkc.com

ISBN: 0-9719295-0-5

All Rights Reserved.
This publication is protected by Copyright and permission should be obtained from the Publisher prior to any prohibited reproduction, storage in a retrieval system, or transmission in any form or by any means, electronic, mechanical, photocopying, recording, or otherwise.

Printed in the United States of America

TABLE OF CONTENTS

Table of Contents .... i-iii

Index to Analysis of Letters iv

Foreword v

Biography of F. W. Tamblyn .... vi-x

Preface 3

To the student 4

        Method of Practice 4

        Deep Breathing 4

        Writing Material 5-6

        Position of Body at Desk 7-9

        Speed 11

        Movements 11

        Standard Alphabet 12

        Principles 13-4

Business Writing 15

        The Beginning - Process of Muscular Development 16-17

        Letter Forms and Practice 23-64

Sentence Practice	65-72
Form Study and Supplementary Movement Exercises	73-80
Business Writing Transparency Form	after 80
Artistic Writing	81
Movement, Material, Adjusting Holder, Position	82-83
Letter Forms and Practice	84-108
Signature Writing	109
Variations of Letter Forms	110-111
Card Writing	112-114
Artistic Writing Transparency Form	after 114
Engravers Script	115
Letter Forms	115-118
Sample	119
Lettering and Engrossing	120
Illustrating Pencil Outlining	120
Medieval Lettering	121
Engrossers' Text	121
Marking	122
Broad Pen Roman	123
Vertical and Slant Gothic	123

Modified Old English 124
Broad Pen and Fine Pen Gothic... 125
Fine Pen Roman 126
Old English 127
Free-Hand Gothic 128
Gothic 129
Roman... 130
Variety of Styles 131-132
Resolution Samples 133
Tamblyn Business Card 134
Flourishing Techniques 135
Basic Bird Strokes 135
Position 136
Flourishing Samples 137-144
Fancy Pen Work of F. W. Tamblyn.. 145-170

INDEX TO ANALYSIS OF LETTERS.

Business Writing.

Small letters	a	b	c	d	e	f	g	h	i	j	k	l	m
Page	42	48	42	43	42	49	46	48	43	46	49	47	41
	n	o	p	q	r	s	t	u	v	w	x	y	z
	41	42	45	45	44	44	43	41	43	43	42	45	47

Figures pages 50, 51, and 73.

Capitals	A	B	C	D	E	F	G	H	I	J	K	L	M
Page	52	52	53	53	54	54	55	55	56	56	57	57	58
	N	O	P	Q	R	S	T	U	V	W	X	Y	Z
	58	59	59	60	60	61	61	62	62	63	63	64	64

Further Form Illustrations and Analysis on Pages 73 and 74, and Transparent Forms, Page 81.

Artistic Writing.

Small letters	a	b	c	d	e	f	g	h	i	j	k	l	m
Page	87	100	87	96	92	100	100	100	92	92	100	100	87
	n	o	p	q	r	s	t	u	v	w	x	y	z
	87	87	96	92	87	87	96	92	87	92	96	100	96

Figures page 106.

Capitals	A	B	C	D	E	F	G	H	I	J	K	L	M
Page	98	90	94	98	98	90	105	94	105	105	90	94	85
	N	O	P	Q	R	S	T	U	V	W	X	Y	Z
	85	98	90	105	102	94	90	102	102	85	85	102	108

Transparent Forms in Back of Book.

Foreword to F. W. Tamblyn's Home Instructor in Penmanship

It has been sixty-three years since the seventh edition of F. W. Tamblyn's Home Instructor in Penmanship was published. Some three generations ago, when life revolved around different things of importance - one of which that was foremost -- handwriting.

The purpose of this book is to teach and inspire. To put you back in touch with what was commonplace some 100 years ago. Back then your career would be dependent upon your abilities as a penman. No ballpoint pens, typewriters, word processors or computers would have been available to you. To be able to write well and legibly would help you to secure your position in life.

It is with great admiration that we bring you this book as it was originally published. Some forty-four additional pieces of original art created by F. W. Tamblyn that have never been published before are also included in this, the revised Eighth Edition.

As we strive to emulate the work of the masters we need to keep in mind that times back then were different from what we now experience. Pen nibs were made from fine steels and honed by skilled craftsmen. The antique nibs we find today are cherished for their abilities and are no longer in the mainstream of life. Papers were made and finished for use with these nibs and the inks of the day. Superb fine lines and strong dark elegant shades could be achieved by the skilled penman.

We would have been schooled properly in handwriting techniques. And if we wanted to take up these techniques as a profession there would have been numerous ways to learn the art form. Correspondence courses were abundant and the Tamblyn course was one of the premier programs available. We could have chosen from numerous schools to study this vocation. The Zanerian College in Columbus, Ohio was held up by many to be the foremost place to develop the needed skills to last a lifetime career.

We wish you well in your endeavors as you study these pages astutely. Practice using a light hand and proper technique. Learn to mix and match your papers, inks and nibs to the job at hand. Be assured that the techniques you will find in these pages will serve you well. They were developed from the teaching of the late 1800s and F. W. Tamblyn's life experiences over a 49-year period of time.

The Publishers: Ziller of Kansas City, Richard J. and Vivian A. Mungall

A Biography of the Life and Times of
F. W. (Frederick William) Tamblyn
January 4, 1870 -- February 16, 1947

Master Penman Frederick W. Tamblyn, or "F. W.", as he liked to be known, was born on a farm near Sugar, Kansas in 1870. His parents emigrated from Cornwall England to this Miami county town loacted in eastern Kansas in 1868. His older brother was born in England, but died soon after arriving in Kansas.

Tamblyn's early education was in the local District School. His chores and regular farm work consumed most of his spare time. As with many, the life of a pioneer farmer made an impression upon him. Its pleasures and hardships helped to shape his choices of what to do with his life. An interest in penmanship began to develop at about age 11.

When Tamblyn was 16 years of age, he encountered an itinerant teacher of handwriting named Mr. Goss whose pen flourishes captivated the young Tamblyn. Tamblyn's father arranged for him to attend classes, lessons that sparked a lasting fire and helped to focus his ambition on becoming a professional penman. Most all of his spare time was devoted to the practicing of handwriting. His sources of inspiration and technique came from publications of the time such as Gaskell's Guide, The Western Penman, and The Penman's Art Journal.

When Tamblyn finished District School he attended the Paola, Kansas High School. On finishing there, he entered Central Business College in Sedalia, Missouri where he graduated with a grade of 99% in each of his ten subjects. In nine months from the time he entered the college, he was hired as a teacher for the college. He taught there for five years.

Tamblyn left the school in the fall of 1894. Using his own instruction book, he organized and taught classes throughout the country, in essence, following the footsteps of Mr. Goss by becoming an itinerant penman. With the unexpected death of his father in the winter of 1894, Tamblyn returned to the family farm to help his mother close up the affairs of the farm and relocate her to a place in town.

In September 1895, he was teaching at Southwestern Business College in St. Louis, Missouri, where he remained for a year. He then established his own studio for engrossing art and diplomas as well as, the Tamblyn School of Penmanship - a correspondence course. Just before leaving Sedalia, he had begun to take students by mail. He believed that he was the first to attempt to teach penmanship by corresponding with the student through the mail. His approach was to use actual pen written copies, typed instructions, and red ink criticisms. This format lasted him some 50 years. We estimate that approximately 40,000 students from all parts of the world have taken the course.

After two years in St. Louis, Tamblyn, wanting to be nearer his mother and his home, moved to Kansas City, Missouri on July 1, 1897. Some of his business followed him from St. Louis and he gained new business in Kansas City. With the gradual growth of the correspondence teaching he soon found himself to be quite busy. Tamblyn was quoted as having said, "I've been on the jump ever since."

Shortly after moving to Kansas City, he was employed by the Brown Business College where he taught penmanship classes. Once his own business began to occupy all of his time, he left the college to pursue his business interests. At this time he took up residence at 3620 Walnut Street and established his studio in the Ridge Building in Kansas City.

F.W. Tamblyn and Florence Francis were married in 1900 and had two children. William, who was born in 1903, died of peritonitis resulting from an operation for appendicitis in 1922. With the untimely death of his only son, William at the age of 18, Tamblyn was almost overcome with grief and disappointment. He had planned to train his son to take over the penmanship business when he was ready to retire. His daughter, Francis, was born in 1910 and became a dress designer. She married B. C. Bell and eventually moved to Chicago. Her family subsequently relocated to St. Louis with their two children.

In April, 1902, Tamblyn wrote an article for The Educator, a business publication. Some of his observations and philosophies follow in his words:

"All of us who have made any pretensions in the field of penmanship, know more or less of my subject, some more, some less, doubtless. And while a few may obtain their knowledge from theory only, the most of us have drunk from the fount of experience. A penman who has been in the work for only a short time, can scarcely have failed to have been called upon to execute a piece of engrossing, and if located in a city the calls upon him, doubtless, have been quite frequent. It is needless for me to urge upon the profession, a knowledge of this line of work, for all are aware of its utility as a side line for the business college teacher, if not exactly familiar with it as a profession of itself. It is as a profession that I shall treat it. Many of the principal cities have those who follow Engrossing as a business, and the success achieved compels us to class it as one of the honorable and remunerative occupations of life."

"The old adage, 'Art is long and time is fleeting,' reminds us that it must be begun in youth; old age is too late; middle age is too late."

".....hard work added to the innate love and ardent desire... ..will make of any young man a fair success. However, they with natural ability will make the shinning lights."

".....to make a successful Engrosser, I would say that you need to be able to execute well the following: Script, Spencerian, Copper Plate, many styles of lettering, as many as twenty at least among the most important I would name, Old English, of various styles, German Text, Marking, Roman, and Sickles, as well as other ornamental letters....and should be a sketch artist, brush artist and skillful with all manner of ornamental designs."

"As a word to young penmen.....I would picture the road to success briefly as follows: hard work, incessant study, love for the work, a clear and high ideal, indomitable courage, stubborn will, time, and above all hard work. What obstacles will hard work not surmount, and one victory gained is but an additional weapon with which to fight the next. What a satisfaction, what self-gratification to see our efforts prosper, and a profession with humble beginning gradually grows year by year into a business with such volume, that we are crowded to handle it."

Tamblyn first began using magazines for promoting his correspondence courses in 1910. His philosophy was that a volume of business at a fair price was the key to success. For many years he spent from $300 to $1,000 a month in advertising, with enrollments running from 200 to 400 per month. With the decline of business in the late twenties he decreased his advertising. However, he never stopped using it as a tool to develop new business.

His labor intensive "fresh from the pen" copies were sent to his students along with an occasional letter of inspiration urging the students to do their very best work on every lesson.

For over 30 years, diplomas for high schools were inscribed by him. Working at his rolltop desk, he prepared penmanship copy books for business colleges and art schools, inscribed memorial parchments eulogizing prominent men, including the late William Rockhill Nelson (a Kansas City businessman and philanthropist), Warren Harding (see page 133), Woodrow Wilson, and several other presidents, and produced a plaque that was presented to Queen Marie of Romania when she visited Kansas City in 1926 (see page 133). He also testified in trials as a handwriting expert.

F. W. Tamblyn was described as always being a hard worker who possessed good judgement, was honest, sincere and always endeavored to give students and customers full value and more where possible. His combined business and art abilities led to financial success and contributed to society by starting thousands on the road to better penmanship.

Tamblyn was fortunate in securing the services of Stephen A. Ziller, a 1932 graduate of the Zanerian College in Columbus, Ohio. Tamblyn contacted Parker Bloser at The Zaner-Bloser Company to place an ad for a professional penman. On Bloser's advice, Ziller contacted Tamblyn. On January 1, 1933 Ziller came to Kansas City and started to work on the same day by showing Tamblyn his lettering skills. Tamblyn found him a reputable boarding house and even tested the bed.

Ziller was a good designer and fine engrosser with considerable ability. Together Tamblyn and Ziller labored for nearly five years. A good share of their success was attributed to Ziller's ability and industry. In 1936, Tamblyn wanted to partially retire, and Ziller wanted to take over the business. So, they came to an agreement that set Ziller on a course of running the operation for the next 55 years.

As a result of the business conditions in the 1930s, Tamblyn and Ziller began to devote greater attention to engrossing and diplomas. After the depression of the early thirties, the manufacturing of diplomas began using the newly developed technique of lithograhy. This part of the business grew and caught the attention of his competition - the older and larger companies in Chicago, Illinois, Wichita, Kansas, Houston, Texas and St. Paul, Minnesota. They offered lithographed sheepskin and paper diplomas which were personalized. In their bindery, they produced all kinds of diploma covers and handsomely embossed covers made from steer hide.

Continuing in Tamblyn's footsteps, Ziller wrote and published his own five book series in 1946 to be used for the newly updated correspondence courses. He covered the subjects of Business Writing, Artistic Writing, Card Writing, Engrossing and Flourishing. Along with his books he wrote a small "how to" booklet with examples to accompany each of the five courses. Ziller continued offering the correspondence courses until the courses became too labor intensive with individual critiques. Ziller's important historical five book series, At Home With Artistic Penwork is still in print.

In the declining years of his life Tamblyn was asked about his formula for success. His reply was, "Service." And he believed that there were still great opportunities for both young men and women to succeed as at any time in the past.

It was said that the whole secret is embodied in the following qualities: brains and hard work in the use of them, with diligent use of both hands and feet, personality, faithfulness, sincerity, honesty, ability and thorough qualification in the chosen profession, rendering if possible, greater service than competitors. In other words, "more for less." Remembering that volume with small individual profit is essential to financial success.

During the Christmas rush of 1944, while wrapping a large bundle with strong cord, Tamblyn made a quick hard pull to break the string when something "snapped" in his shoulder. His writing hand became numb and excruciating pain resulted, leaving him unable to letter. Thus, the man who had known no limit in his ambition to serve the public with his penwork would now experience a physical limitation. He eventually developed arthritis in that arm. It was written that the Tamblyn name and work would live on as long as penmanship continued to be a profession. In fact, Tamblyn's name endures even now, long after the profession of penmanship was lost to the sands of time.

Having been in poor health for several years, Tamblyn had undergone several operations before his passing. On February 16, 1947, Frederick W. Tamblyn passed away at Research Hospital in Kansas City, Missouri. At the time he was residing at 2 East 58th Street and was buried in the Forest Hill Cemetery located in

Kansas City.

In an admiring memory, reflecting on his passing at the age of 77, an article was headlined, "Tamblyn, the Beloved Penman is Dead" and it was acknowledged that the profession had lost one its greatest masters. For over 50 years the name of Tamblyn, the Penman and his well known advertisement: "'Learn to Write' I can make a good penman of you at home during spare time. Write for my free book 'How to become a Good Penman'... Your name will be elegantly written on a card if you enclose a stamp." F.W. Tamblyn believed "that the price of success is measured by inspiration, application, and perspiration." As a penman and teacher he ranks among the finest Master Penmen.

It is the opinion of S.A. Ziller that Tamblyn was one of the finest business writing and ornamental penmen in the country. His style had a precise symmetric roundness to it that was in the same class as Palmer, Zaner and Spencer.

With his talent and abilities, F.W. Tamblyn spent a career teaching and putting pen to paper to relate for others such terms as: "This Diploma is granted to.....", "With all the rights and privileges appertaining thereto.....", "In grateful appreciation.....", "With profound regret.....", This tribute is given to.....", "Whereas, resolved.....", and "In memory of.....".

Frederick William Tamblyn was one of the most widely known penmen in the country and had successful students in many different countries. It was said that all who knew him could honestly say, "There was a man who served his profession long and well, and was a great credit to it."

Reference Sources:

1. The Blue Book: Containing Photographs and Sketches of a Few Commercial Teachers, L. E. Stacy, The Tribune Publishing Company, 1907.

2. The Educator, The Zaner-Bloser Company, Columbus, Ohio, "The Penman-Artist and Business Educator - Engrossing", by F. W. Tamblyn, Kansas City, MO, April, 1902.

3. The Educator, The Zaner-Bloser Company, Columbus, Ohio, F. W. (Frederick William) Tamblyn, "Flowers to the Living" by Adjt. F. O. Anderson, Hibbing, Minnesota, January, 1945, page 22.

4. The Educator, The Zaner-Bloser Company, Columbus, Ohio, "Tamblyn, the Beloved Penman is Dead", by Major F. O. Anderson, April, 1947, page 14.

5. The Kansas City Star, Kansas City, Missouri., February 17, 1947, page 6.

6. The Tamblyn Engrossing Art Studio and School of Penmanship. Various materials.

7. Ziller, Stephen Anthony, Cincinnati, Ohio. 2001

8. Ziller of Kansas City Engrossing Art Studio. Various materials.

PREFACE.

THE PURPOSE of this book is to teach rapid, easy and practical business handwriting. It is designed to be of assistance to the teacher of penmanship in his class work, and particularly helpful to those students who have not the opportunity of placing themselves under the instruction of a practical teacher of writing.

The Tamblyn System is based on Muscular movement; by some designated as "Arm Movement" and by others as "Forearm Movement;" which is the only movement that has ever produced practical business writers. While the copies represent a fair degree of accuracy, yet mechanical accuracy, such as used in some copy books, is purposely avoided. Such mechanical accuracy of copies restricts movement and develops pure finger action.

It has been thoroughly proven that practice from copies mechanically accurate develops a cramped movement. It compels finger action in the formation of letters, giving a fair degree of accuracy in slow writing, and which, when speed is necessary, becomes scribbling, almost illegible. In the Tamblyn System, movement is placed first, accuracy of form secondary.

The lifelessness and mechanical exactness of hand engraved copies which represent the skill of the penciler and engraver instead of the penman, do not arouse the enthusiasm of the pupil, and tend rather to discourage than to encourage him. On the other hand copies that show they were executed easily and have the appearance of real writing, encourage him with the idea that he will be able to write similarly with reasonable effort and practice.

The exercises and copies given in this book are photo-engraved from actual free hand, rapid writing by the author and are, therefore, an exact representation; and the system is practically the same (with some changes as experience has taught) as employed by him for the past thirty-five years in class work and in correspondence instruction.

TO THE STUDENT.

THE following lessons will make of you a good penman, if you follow instructions implicitly. The average time to acquire such a handwriting is from four to six months, practicing an hour or so a day. Practice regularly every day, if you want the best results. Two practice periods of thirty minutes each are better than one period of sixty minutes.

Read all instructions carefully, thoughtfully, re-read them, lest some important point may be overlooked. Practice studiously, carefully, yet with sufficient life and vigor to produce smooth and artistic lines. Better inaccurate writing with smooth, graceful lines, than accurate writing with weak, stiff, shaky lines.

Smooth, graceful lines can only be made with a rapid movement.
Be a close critic of the results of your practice.

Do not expect to revolutionize your writing in a few days. Improvement will be slow at first. If you have to acquire muscular movement you will likely form the letters poorer after a month's practice than at first, so do not become discouraged if it seems you are going backward. Changing from a cramped finger movement to a free movement is certain to lose control of the hand for a time, but it should not last long; then as you begin to get control again the lines are smooth and you have a foundation laid for a practical handwriting.

Do not, under any circumstances, permit yourself to go back to finger movement after you have once undertaken the muscular movement, no matter how hard it may seem to form readable letters. All will come out right if instructions are implicitly followed.

METHOD OF PRACTICE.

Practice methodically and studiously—not carelessly and listlessly. Practice regularly, some every day, if possible. Resolve first to acquire a free movement; second, a light touch; and third, to gain control of it. Make all practice sheets **NEAT**; study arrangement and neatness. Begin each line an equal distance from the edge of the paper, and space equally, so that in writing line after line, of the same copy, the words will be directly under each other. It is suggested that you write line after line of the same copy until from one-third of a page to a full page is written. You are particularly cautioned to avoid HAPHAZARD PRACTICE—particularly the habit of writing a few words of one copy and a few of another, and so on, until dozens have been tried. Take them in the order given, devoting sufficient time to each to show some definite improvement.

DEEP BREATHING.

A good circulation of air means good circulation of blood. It means better nerves, more energy, improved health, so if you will take at least ten deep breaths every day, filling your lungs to the very bottom, you will be healthier, stronger, and less susceptible to disease.

It is suggested to the penmanship student that he straighten up about every 30 minutes, throw the head and shoulders back, and take a few full, deep breaths, filling the lungs to their full capacity, thus ridding them of any cobwebs that may accumulate.

Writing Material

USE THE BEST that can be had. Good paper, good pens and good ink.

PENS.

Use a medium fine-pointed pen in beginning to learn the movement, also a pen that is elastic. It is a known fact that good writing cannot be executed with a heavy movement. Students who have been using finger movement, almost invariably use a heavy movement unawares. To overcome this, an elastic pen is recommended, so that the pupil can easily see the touch he is using. If he be bearing heavily on the pen, it will, as a consequence, make a heavy mark. If he uses a light movement, the pen will accordingly make a light mark. After a light movement is obtained, use any pen desired. Some prefer a coarse pen for business writing, while others prefer a fine pen. It is a matter that no definite rule can be given for, and must be determined by the fancy and judgment of the person writing, his surrounding circumstances, etc.

PAPER.

Foolscap, legal cap, letter paper, or any flat paper ruled, of good surface, 8 or 8½ inches wide, will answer the purpose. Avoid using small note paper. The older paper is the better it is for pen work. Always endeavor to get a paper that has firm and hard surface. Generally the cheap paper is not worth having. It is almost a waste of time, and in many cases entirely such, to use it. In practicing on any kind of paper do not be afraid of writing over it too many times. After writing across one way, turn it and write across the opposite. Then, if so disposed, turn it and write across obliquely. In most cases amateurs do their best writing the second or third time going over the paper. The first time they are intimidated by a feeling of fear that they will make some mistake in the work, when they want to make everything just about right. But when practicing over paper that has already been written on, this feeling disappears and they start out with a bold and strong movement, not affected by "Buck Ague," and really learn more about form, movement and penmanship generally than is possible to be learned in going over it the first time. Do not be afraid of using paper. Those who have become good penmen have used **thousands** of sheets of paper.

INK.

Any ink that flows freely will answer. The common blue and green writitng fluids are probably more generally used than others; however, it is hard to beat black ink.

PEN HOLDER.

The straight holder is most generally used, although the oblique holder is preferred by many. It throws the pen more squarely on the point; and for shaded writing it should be used exclusively.

Select a holder of medium size, neither extremely small, nor extremely large. Almost any kind will do, except those having polished metal at the bottom. They are too slick to hold easily.

CARE OF PEN.

TEEL PENS, as they come from the factory, are covered with a varnish to keep them from rusting or corroding. This varnish is of a greasy nature, and must of necessity be wiped from the pen before ink will flow from it freely. To remove this varnish, wet a piece of soft paper or cloth with the mouth and wipe the pen carefully before dipping it in the ink. Do not be afraid of getting too much ink on the pen. Do not barely touch the ink with the point of the pen, but dip it on in, filling the pen up to the eye. Scarcely anything is more amusing than to see one just barely touching the pen to ink, then taking it out and giving it a dash through the air, throwing off on the floor most of what little ink was at first on the pen. By having the pen full of ink, it works very much better. Always wipe the pen off carefully when through writing, and when dirty ink is being used the pen should also be wiped quite frequently.

No rule can be given regarding the length of time a pen should be used. It all depends upon the amount of writing done, the kind of paper used, the one doing the writing, the quality of the pen when taken from the box and the kind of ink used. Acid writing fluid corrodes a pen rapidly. Some pens can be used several days, while others from the same box won't last two minutes, and even some are worthless when taken from the box. They often, in some way, get sprung, and when they do they are worthless; throw them away without wasting time with them. Don't be **stingy** with pens.

HOW TO KEEP INK IN GOOD ORDER.

By long standing and evaporation it often becomes entirely too thick to flow, and when such is the case water must be added to thin it. Add only a little at a time, until the desired thickness is obtained. Always keep the bottle or inkstand closed when not in use, so as to keep out particles of dirt. Good work absolutely cannot be done with dirty ink. It must be clean and clear, so that hair lines will be **regular**, thus presenting an artistic appearance.

HOW TO INSERT PENS IN HOLDER.

In a straight holder, push the pen in until the point sticks out from ¾ of an inch to 1 inch.

In the oblique holder, the rule most generally known and probably the most correct of all, is to insert it in such a way that the point of the pen will be in an exact line with the center of the stock of the holder, when sighted down from the top to bottom. This, however, consumes some time. A good way to do is as follows:

Place the thumb of the left hand against the back part of the metal, and with the right hand shove the pen in until it strikes the thumb against the metal. The end of the pen is then even with the back part of the metal, and by this method the pen will always be in the same position, which is a necessity in order to do good work.

POSITION OF BODY AT DESK.

SIT EXACTLY facing the desk; left side slightly closer to it, with the breast an inch or two from the edge of the desk; both arms on the table and resting at about right angles with each other. (See illustrations No. 1 below and No. 3, page 9.) Sit moderately straight and in leaning over, be sure not to bend the spine between the neck and hips. (See illlustrations, No. 2 below, and No. 6, page 9.) Don't crowd the chair up under the desk, neither sit on the very front edge of the seat. This compels the curving of the spine, else sitting uncomfortably straight. Rest any necessary weight of the body on the left arm, thus not interfering with the freedom of the right arm.

HEIGHT OF TABLE OR DESK.

The top of the desk should be from 30 to 31 inches from the floor, and about 12 to 13 inches from the seat of the chair for the average person of from 5 feet 5 inches to 5 feet 10 inches in height. Persons shorter or taller should vary this distance accordingly. Observe this rule closely. Never use a desk or table too high, nor one too low. Square tables are always better than round ones, and it should be large enough to permit the elbows to rest on it. The smoother and more even the top, the better.

POSITION OF THE FEET.

There is no positive position recommended for the feet, except to keep them on the floor. After you get the other positions correct the position of the feet won't matter much. The position of them may be shifted occasionally, to rest.

POSITION OF PAPER.

APER should lie obliquely on the table. Hold it so that the line on the **paper can be kept with ease.** This can be determined by moving the hand across the sheet, and if the pen touches both ends of the same line on the paper the position is correct. (See illustration No. 3, opposite page.) Be careful, however, to keep the top of the paper turned well to the right. This will make the writing straighter, and experience teaches that nine-tenths of the students of penmanship write entirely too slanting. Always keep from three to six sheets of paper under the sheet upon which you are writing. Never put a book or crumpled newspaper under it. The surface on which you are writing must be firm and solid, and not so high from the table as to leave edges for the wrist to reach over. Never roll practice paper when it can be avoided. If paper in tablet form is used for practice, **tear out a few sheets rather than write on the thick pad.**

POSITION OF RIGHT ARM AND HAND.

The right arm should rest on the table so the end of the elbow projects over the edge of the table. **(See illustration No. 3 on opposite page.)** The forearm should lie on the table in a diagonal position and resting freely, so that motion in all directions may be obtained with the greatest ease.

The hand should rest loosely and slide either on the **nail** or **first joint** of the little finger (on the nail, if inclined to stick to the paper or desk.) It may also slide on the bulge at end of wrist, unless the hand sweats so that it sticks, in which case the only rest should be the nail of the little finger. (See illustrations 4, 5, 6, 8 and 9.)

POSITION OF LEFT ARM AND HAND.

The uses of the left arm and hand are not generally recognized or thought to amount to much. This is a mistaken idea. Its functions are just as great and its co-operation as all-essential as that of the right hand. It should lie on the table as the right arm, except pointing in the opposite diagonal direction. On this arm should rest any weight of the body that there may be resting on either arm, so as to leave the right arm free to act. The left hand should hold and guide the paper so as to make it convenient for the right hand. Use the fingers of the left hand nimbly in holding and moving the paper. With it pull the paper from left to right, up and down, etc., to suit the position and movement of the right hand. (See illustration 3, opposite.)

WRIST.

One of the most important features regarding position is that of the wrist. The top of the wrist should slant slightly downward toward the right (outside). Avoid much slant. Do not turn it up on edge. It should be nearly flat enough to hold a coin on top while writing. (See illustrations Nos. 4, 5 and 6 opposite.)

The ball of the wrist may touch if there is no tendency to stick and drag, but if there is the least such tendency hold it slightly up. (See illustrations 4, 6 and 9.)

Hold the hand straight with **the forearm, or even turn it** slightly **to the right,** but **never** turn it to the left, ("pigeon-toe.") (See illustration 5.)

—8—

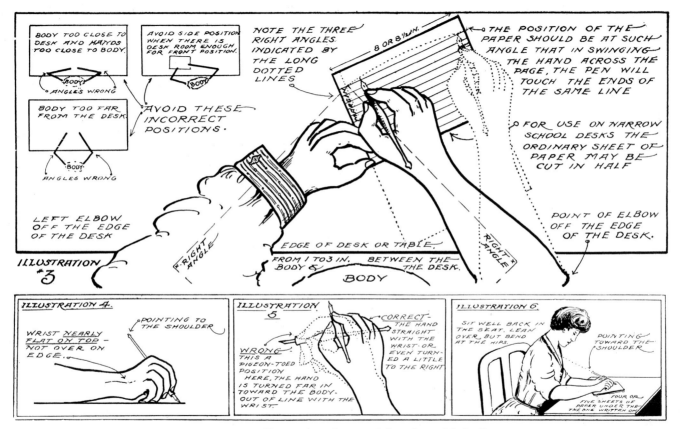

Self explanatory illustrations for careful study and imitation.

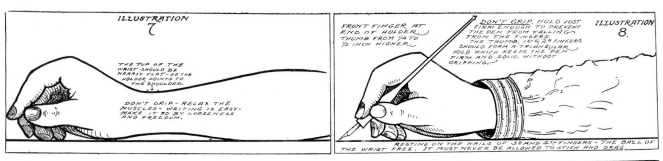
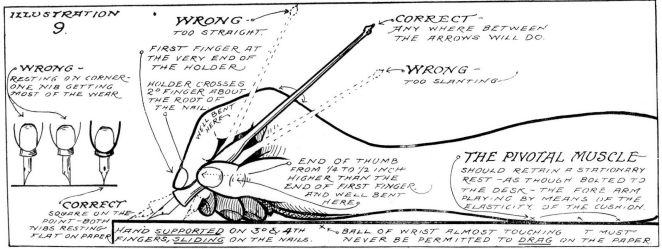

Study and imitate these self explanatory illustrations.

CLOTHING FOR THE RIGHT ARM

Should be thin and loose. The best work can be done with the arm bare or with one loose sleeve. There are those who assert that it is all a matter of habit; that one can write just as well with all sleeves on the arm as off, if he but accustom himself to it. It is not true. It is a good plan to pull the undershirt sleeve above the elbow, else cut it off.

SPEED.

Speed is very essential to good writing. It is generally conceded that movement is the foundation of good writing, yet movement can never be acquired without considerable speed. Don't imagine you can acquire a good handwriting by a drawing process. All lines must be made with sufficient speed to make them smooth and clear cut. Remember this: **Rapid motion produces smooth lines, and slow motion produces shaky and wabbly lines.**
The approximate speed desired is indicated beneath most of the following copies. It is not possible for every one to acquire the same speed, but considerable latitude is given, and it is expected you will practice earnestly to approximate the speed indicated.

DON'T GUESS AT THE SPEED—CONSULT THE WATCH.

Don't feel discouraged if you have only about half the speed required. You can develop speed quickly. Don't think much about Formation while working for speed. Get speed and motion first, then look after Form later.
Movement, speed, and a light line **first**; Form second. To reverse this order is like "Hitching the cart before the horse."

COUNTING.

Both teacher and pupil should count in making exercises and movement drills. The counts may be for each down stroke or for each completed letter, as preferred. One count for a letter is probably the better for such letters as a, n, m, u, w, and c; as to count for each down stroke requires very rapid counting, else too slow writing.

MOVEMENTS.

There are four movements: Muscular (or Forearm); Finger; Combined, and Whole Arm.
Muscular Movement: The arm rests on the large muscle below the elbow, which muscle or rest acts as a pivot on which all motion rolls. The only other rest is the nails of the third and fourth fingers, which slide in unison with the pen. The power to move the hand and pen emanates from the large muscles of the body.
Finger Movement: The only action is from the wrist, out.
Combined Movement: A union of Muscular and Finger movements. The fingers move very much the same as in Finger movement (particularly in making small letters), only not so much, the wrist and finger rests are **movable**, not **stationary**. Most writers who **claim** to use Muscular movement **really** use Combined.
Whole Arm: The only rest for the arm is the fingers, otherwise free from the table, swinging in the air. It is tiresome and seldom used.

—11—

STANDARD ALPHABET.

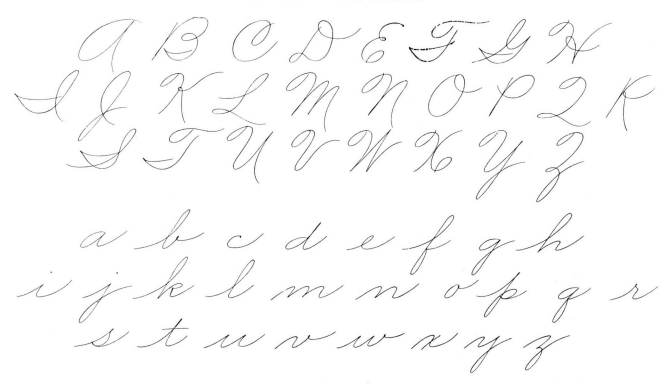

The above forms are used in the copies of this book. Slight variations are permissible.

TOUCH

The touch should be uniformly light. The **down** stroke should be as light as the **up** stroke, and both as light as the pen you use will make without pressure. The coarser the pen the heavier the stroke, of course, but avoid pressure on it. Support the weight of the hand with the finger rest. See illustration, page 10.

FORM

Don't give **much** attention to form, until an easy **muscular movement** and a **light touch** have been established. However, from the beginning observe and try to follow the correct forms of "a" and "o" below. The same applies also to "d," "g," and "q." The crossing of "t" and dot and period should be followed. Then when movement and touch are getting natural, form becomes really important. Study and compare with your copies, observe the instruction attached to letters, pages 41 to 64. Also read pages 73 and 74, and compare your letters frequently with the Transparent Forms in the back of this book.

A **STRAIGHT LINE** extends uniformly in one direction without bend or kink.

A **RIGHT CURVE** is a line that curves out to the right of a straight line.

A **LEFT CURVE** is a line that curves out to the left of a straight line

A **COMPOUND CURVE** is a combination of both a Right and Left curve, beginning with either and ending with the other.

A **VANISHING HAIR LINE** is a stroke made by picking up the pen quickly while in motion—not by an abrupt stop.

The above lines and curves are occasionally used in explanations and instructions following.

Note very carefully the illustrations and explanations above.

—13—

THINGS TO DO

Use a desk or table about 30 inches high.
Study the illustrations carefully.
Read instructions beneath the copies.
Read, thoughtfully, intelligently, **and remember it.**
Try to do things as you understand.
Wipe a new pen before using.
Keep the right arm down tight on the desk.
Make your motto "Others have, I will."
The eyes should be from 10 to 14 inches from the point
of pen.
Keep the pen clean.
Keep a swinging, and rolling motion.
Be a severe critic.
Keep the eyelet of the pen on top (not to either side.)
Practice **daily, and think** as your practice.
Use ruled paper 8 or 8½ inches wide.
Make the down strokes as light as the up strokes.
Consult the transparent Form sheet frequently.
Remember figures are as important as letters.
For correct spacing of words see page 32.
Work,—there is no royal road to **good writing.**
Movement **FIRST,** Touch **Second,** Form **Third.**
Review past lessons a few minutes each day. Generally
30 to 60 minutes practice periods are best, unless
you can practice longer with interest and without
tiring.
Generally more improvement will result from two prac-
tice periods of 45 minutes each than from one period
of an hour and a half.
Think—Study—many failures result from lack of these.
Read—and **reread** instructions carefully—you must un-
derstand before you can hope to do.
Try to maintain uniform slant.
For **less** slant, turn top of paper to the **right.**
For **more** slant, turn top of paper to the **left.**
Keep your writing on the line.
Put force, speed and dash behind the pen.
Use both sides of paper in your practice.
Relax—Muscles and joints should work freely.
Practice movement drills, pages 76 to 80, frequently.

DON'T'S

Don't expect to become a good penman in a week.
Don't lean against the desk.
Don't grip the holder.
Don't use a scratchy or badly worn pen.
Don't bear on the pen.
Don't become unreasonably careless.
Don't allow the arm to **slide** on the desk.
Don't use a holder with polished metal tip.
Don't hesitate, let the hand go.
Don't change around too much.
Don't hold the pen on the corner. (See illustration on
pages 9 and 10.)
Don't let the hand roll over on edge.
Don't allow the wrist to stick nor drag.
Don't use dirty ink.
Don't give up; keep trying.
Don't write on top of a tablet. Have only a few sheets
underneath.
Don't hook nor loop small a, o, d, g, nor q.
Don't make lines for dots and periods.
Don't make curves in crossing "t."
Don't hump the back of small b, h, f, k, and l.
Don't be absent minded. Concentrate.
Don't fail to time your speed by the watch occasionally.
Don't compromise with Finger Movement. Be sure to use
muscular.
Don't permit carelessness — neither be so careful as to
cramp your movement.
Don't dissipate, nor lose much sleep and expect steady
nerves.
Don't run lower loops into one space letters on the line
below.
Don't quite touch the line above with any letter, either
capital or small.
Don't "pigeon-toe" the hand by bending inward at the
wrist. Keep it **straight,** or turn **outward—never in-
ward.**
Don't **draw,** but **write,** freely, easily.
Don't tolerate a slow, cramped movement.
Don't write **excessively** large, nor **excessively** small.

—14—

Business Writing

MOVEMENT must be developed thoroughly, as it positively is the foundation of good writing, either plain or ornamental; the keystone to the arch of chirographic attainment. Lack of movement is the main cause of the great amount of poor writing that now exists; and to carelessness in effort to attain this movement can we attribute the lack of interest that prevails with so many regarding the subject of writing.

It is rather hard for one who for years has been accustomed to a cramped finger movement to break away from it and write with ease and freedom, and if one has acquired the vertical style as taught in some of the public schools, the task seems sometimes almost impossible. But, since we know it must be done if we would acquire a practical handwriting, the best thing to do is to say "I will," and go at it with a vengeance. It should not require more than a month or so to break up finger movement and get fair control of muscular.

Remember, **muscular** movement is the movement necessary for the lessons to follow. Don't compromise with Finger movement. Don't fool yourself into thinking you can acquire Muscular movement by using it during your practice period, and using Finger movement the rest of the day in doing other writing you may have to do. If you go at it that way dismal failure will result. The only safe way is to forever **divorce** yourself from cramped finger movement, **if** you now use it.

Try as earnestly as you may to acquire pure Muscular movement (without any finger action whatever), nine in ten **will retain sufficient Finger movement.**

LESSON 1.

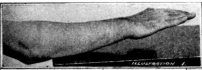

No. 1.— Notice where the arm rests on edge of table. Elbow just off the edge. Keep the arm in this position for all writing, as though nailed or bolted to the table. Instead of moving the arm back as you write down on the sheet, move the sheet upward.

No. 3.— Notice position of the front finger at end of holder, thumb a little higher; holder crossing 2nd finger about the joint; the two smaller fingers doubled under, sliding on the nails, all fingers against each other, and ball of wrist raised above paper

No. 2.— Double up the fist and go through with different movement drills in that position. Then relax by straightening fingers as in No. 1. Interchange these positions frequently for say 3 min. at the beginning of each practice period until your muscles are loose and relaxed.

THE BEGINNING—PROCESS OF MUSCULAR DEVELOPMENT.

Remove surplus clothing from the arm (better remove all); at any rate don't keep more than one thickness over the fore-arm, and **see that it is loose.**

Close the fist and move the hand backward and forward, up and down, rapidly, without slipping or sliding the arm from its rest. See that the arm **rolls** (not **slides**) on the muscles. Go through such gymnastics frequently for five or ten minutes at a time. Rapidly, mind you, as fast as you can make the hand go, and reach as far in all directions as you can without **slipping** the arm.

Study the illustrations (1, 2, 3) above, read the attached explanations, and put the instructions into practice.

Note the scope, or reach, illustrated above. The pivotal rest should not move the least bit in working the arm back and forth. The reach is made by means of the elasticity of the muscle. Should your muscle be tight and inelastic, it will be loosened by the drills as instructed.

LESSON 1. (Continued.)

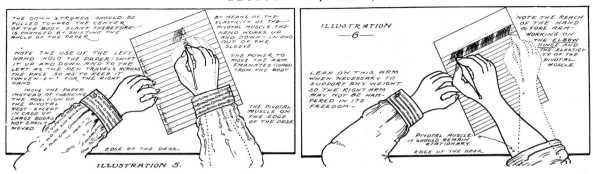

Now, if everything is in readiness for writing, go to work on the straight line (push and pull) exercise below, without the pen in hand at first. Go through the motion rapidly, as fast as you can make the hand fly, reaching as far **forward** and as far **backward** as the elasticity of the muscle will permit. After going through this for several minutes, pick up the pen, ink it, and go to work. Those who are especially awkward with the pen may to good advantage, use a pencil for a few days, until somewhat accustomed to the motion and to the touch.

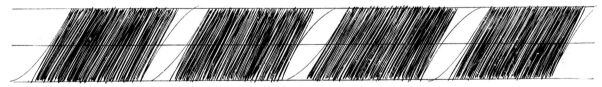

Make two lines high—150 to 200 round trips per minute, which is about as fast as one can count.

Endeavor to make the lines light, whether using the pen or pencil. Also try to get them straight and close together. Don't expect to get them even at top and bottom in the beginning. It will require long practice to do that, but strive particularly for an easy, rapid motion and a light touch. If your watch has a second hand try counting in your mind for 15 seconds until you establish a speed of 40 to 50, then try to apply the same speed to this exercise, not trying to count the exact number of strokes. Watch position of the body, the hand, the pen-holder, and particularly the position of the paper; keep it so that by swinging the hand back and forth, the pen will touch both ends of the same line.

LESSON 2.

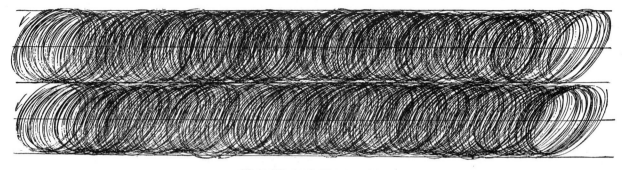

150 to 200 round trips per minute.

    Get all writing material ready, put the arm in proper condition by removing superfluous clothing, so the large **muscle** can move without binding, and undertake the "Running oval" exercise above in real earnest.

    You must swing the pen rapidly in order to get the speed indicated underneath the copy, but it must be **acquired soon.** You may not be able to get it the first few trials, but it will soon come.

    The oval is made with **direct** motion—down on the left up on the right. See the direction by the arrow. It is made 2 spaces high (crossing one ruled line). It is well to start motion and work up speed with pen off the paper. Then drop the pen and keep the lines **light** and very **close together.** Cut out most of the white—not with **heavy** down strokes, but many **light** lines.

    It is not expected you will get them even at top and bottom, neither evenly spaced at first, but you should notice great improvement within a few days. As the pen runs dry, dip and start where you quit, until you have filled the line.

    Make many lines of it during each practice period for the first week or two. Later, it will be well to make a line at the beginning of practice periods. Keep in mind during all your practice on movement drills that it is merely a means to an end. It is similar to diagraming in grammar. These movement drills are not real penmanship in themselves, but necessary for the development of a free and easy motion, which is absolutely necessary for the execution of good writing. Watch your positions—the body, arm, hand, pen and paper. (See pages 7, 8, 9, 10 and 17.)

LESSON 3.

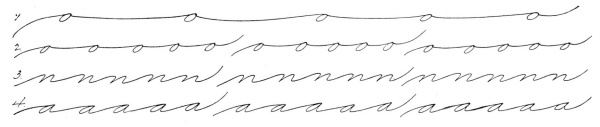

No. 1, 12 to 15 lines. No. 2, 15 to 18 groups. Nos. 3 and 4, 12 to 15 groups per minute.

NOTICE: The line of black face type, like the above, under copies throughout the book, indicates the desired speed per minute. It is put here to be followed, not just to be read and then forgotten or ignored.

So adjust the paper that by swinging the hand back and forth across the page the pen will touch both ends of the same line of ruling, as illustration No. 3, page 9.

The exercise above should be practiced with the idea of developing an easy lateral movement, or rather an easy swing of the hand across the page. The elbow joints should be loose, and swing back and forth like a door with well greased hinges. This is particularly true in practicing copy No. 1. This should be made without lifting the pen until the end of the fifth letter. Notice that the 5 letters fill the line, and try to space them equally. In copies 1, 2, 3 and 4 note that there are three groups of five letters each. Make the arm swing easily and with quite a degree of speed. Be sure the lines are just as light as the pen you are using will make them. The down strokes should not be heavier than the up strokes. The connective line between all three of these letters is a compound curve. See "Principles," page 14. In copy No. 4 bring the last down stroke of the "a" clear to the line before turning off to the next letter. Note carefully the difference between "o" and "a." The "o" is a full oval, egg shaped, while the "a" is considerably more slender. Make all in groups of 5 lines, leaving a blank line between groups; that is, leave every sixth line blank. Count 1, 2, 3, 4, 5, while making all these copies. It is suggested that page after page of each copy be made. As other lessons are taken up, make a group of each, as preliminary movement drill. Time your speed with the watch. (See Lessons 30 and 31 for Forms of these letters). Keep the hand turned well over to the left. (See illustration 4, page 9), so that the pen is **pushed ahead of the hand**, instead of being **pulled after the hand**, as is the case when the hand is thrown over well to the right with the wrist nearly on edge, as shown in illustration 5, page 9.

"There is little difficulty to him who wills."

—19—

LESSON 4.

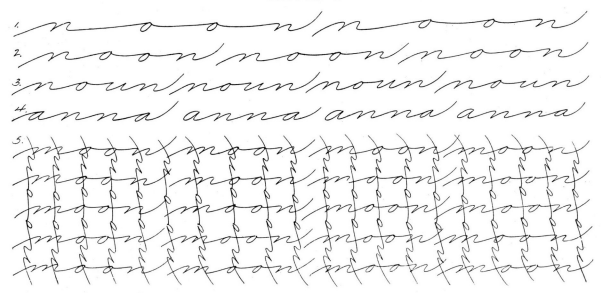

Nos. 1 and 2, 15 to 20 words. Nos. 3 and 4, 18 to 22 words. No. 5, entire exercise, about 3 minutes.

    The copies above are also to develop lateral movement, or motion from left to right. Be sure the arm works easily at the elbow joint. Keep in mind that the o's and a's should be closed at the top, not hooked nor looped, and the "n's" round on top. Nearly all of these connective lines are compound curves, (see "Principles" page 13.) Make in groups of 5 lines, leaving the sixth line blank. Make group after group, several pages of each. .In copy No. 5 write five lines, then turn it around, writing cross ways, putting the letters between the lines just as you see above. I suggest that you spell the word as you write; spelling like this; n-oo-n. Do likewise with the other copies, spelling n-o-u-n, and a-n-n-a. Make the lines absolutely light; down stroke no heavier than the up. Try to keep on the line. Note the speed and time yourself. Be careful to get as nearly the same speed as possible. Watch the position of paper, pen, and body.

LESSON 5.

No. 1 about 15 10 times around. Nos. 2 and 3. about 2½ lines a minute, 6 times around the exercise.

Make copy No. 1 two spaces high on the paper. Note that the ovals are linked into each other, overlapping one-half. Make them as rapidly as indicated above.

Copy No. 2 is the O and oval movement drill. Make them alternately. The O is not a circle, although a full oval. Make the loop at the top rather small (see Form illustration, Lesson 65). By all means watch your movement and if you are not using a perfectly loose and free movement, keep practicing movement exercises persistently until you develop the necessary looseness.

The A in copy No. 3 is more slender than the O. Approximate the speed indicated. Much time may be lost in extra swings in getting motion, before putting the pen on the paper. (See Form illustration, Lesson 51.) Remember, you positively cannot make this letter right unless you make it quickly. If your lines are in any way zigzag, wabbly and heavy, you may be sure you are not using sufficient speed. Write rapidly enough to produce smooth lines. Make copies Nos. 2 and 3 in groups of five lines each, a blank line between groups.

Finish the "A" below the line, with a vanishing hair line. A vanishing line is made by picking up the pen quickly while in motion; not by an abrupt stop. The reason for this is that it assists in keeping the movement. The other finish (upwards) is just as good form, but tends to cramp the movement.

PUT "SNAP" INTO YOUR MOVEMENT.

Don't delude yourself into believing you can become a good writer with a snail-like motion. Finger movement writers will find that speed will injure Form, and that they do not form letters as well as before beginning muscular movement. If proper Form were all that is necessary, it would be discouraging; but Ease and Speed are also necessary requisites of good business writing, hence don't be discouraged, but keep right on using the movement and desired speed, and in due time you will find your hand becoming more and more under control.

—21—

LESSON 6.

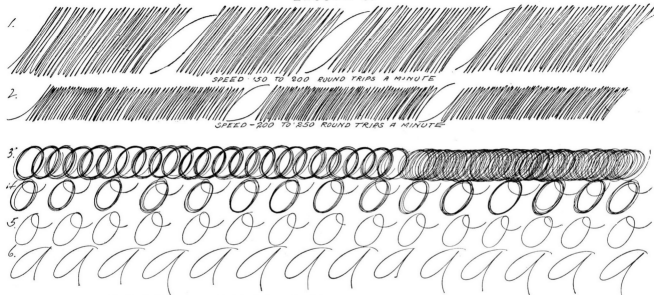

No. 3, 20, 8 times around. No. 4, 16 to 20, 6 times around. Nos. 5 and 6, 60 to 70 per minute.

    More drill on the push and pull exercise. Make copy No. 1 two lines high and close together, cutting out nearly all the white space with numerous lines, not with heavy lines. Strive to make your down strokes as light as the up strokes. Time yourself and see how nearly you approach the speed indicated.

    No. 2 is made one space high and quickly, the same as No. 1. Time yourself on this also.

    Nos. 3, 4, 5 and 6 are practically the same as those for Lesson 5 and the same explanations will answer. The capitals should not quite touch the line above.

    Watch also the position of your paper and swing the arm back and forth across the page occasionally, noting whether the position is such that permits the pen to touch both ends of the same line on the paper. The capitals should fill from 3-4 to 5-6 of the space; not quite touching the line above.

—22—

LESSON 7.

No. 1. about 2½ lines, 6 times around the exercise.   No. 2. 50 to 60.   No. 3, 15 words per minute.

Direct motion exercises. For Form of "C," see Lesson 53, page 53.
In beginning practice on this lesson use the movement drills found in Lessons 5 and 6.
No. 1—Make the movement drills and letters alternately. Go around the oval from 6 to 10 times.
No. 3 completes the entire word without lifting the pen from the paper, keeping in mind the compound connective lines and the round turns on the top of the m's and n's. Quite a degree of speed is necessary to produce smooth, clean-cut lines. Never for one moment let up on your movement and speed; keep them in mind all the time.

LESSON 8.

No. 1. about 2½ lines, 6 times around the exercise.   No. 2, 12 groups.   No. 3, 10 to 12 words per minute.

Direct motion exercises.
In beginning this lesson use movement drills contained in lessons 5 and 6. Make the movement drill of copy No. 1 alternately with the letter. Note that both the **stem** and the **oval** rest on the line; neither should come below nor neither should extend above. (See Lesson 54 for Form explanations.) Go around each oval in the movement drill 6 to 10 times and quite rapidly.
No. 2—Make these in groups of 5 letters, three groups to the line and five lines in a group. Note the speed indicated above and attain it as nearly as possible.
No. 3 is written 3 words to the line, spaced so as to fill the entire line with these words.

— 23 —

LESSON 9.

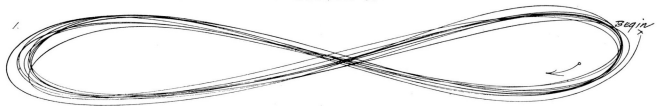

6 per minute, 10 times around.

The entire exercise in about 3 minutes.

No. 1—This is called the figure 8 movement drill. It is a splendid power producer, and should be used frequently. Some find it beneficial in beginning every practice period. Note the point of beginning, and follow the direction of arrow. Make the two ends balance as to size, get lines light, and speed according to that indicated. Use the watch in timing yourself, as it is the only way to determine accurately. Remember the **exact** speed indicated is not expected of every one, but get approximately near it.

No. 2—Use movement drills of copy 3, Lesson 6; and copy 1, Lesson 7, in beginning this copy. The small lettters are connected to the capital, and the word completed without raising the pen. Five words to the line and in groups as shown. Watch the form of small "a" and "n." Time yourself—don't get so slow that your lines become shaky, nor so fast that you lose all control of the hand, and produce a miserable scrawl. Cross-write as illustrated.

LESSON 10.

No. 1 8 or 9 10 times up and down 10 times around. No. 2, 15 to 18 groups. No. 3 15 to 18 words per minute.

Direct motion exercises.

No. 1—This exercise is made two lines high, beginning with the straight lines, which are to be encircled with the oval. Note that the pen is carried from one oval to the next without lifting, until the group is finished.

No. 2—These O's are made in groups of 5 without lifting the pen. Note that there is a double loop in the top which permits of a continuous rolling motion. Make three groups to the line and space equally. Note particularly that there are no sharp turns, that all turns are oval.

No. 3—Four words to the line, and in groups of five lines. Cross practice as in lesson 2, is encouraged. Don't quite touch the lines above with the capitals.

DOTS AND PERIODS.

Special attention is called to the dotting of "i." Make a "dot," not a "line." Place it as high above the "i" as the letter is in height, and directly in line with its slant. A dot is made by setting the pen down and picking it up without moving in any direction on the paper.

Be thoughtful and careful until the correct habit is formed. It doesn't require any real skill to make a dot and a period, and only thoughtful care to place it where it belongs.

QUESTIONS.

Are you following instructions relative to "position," as explained in the beginning? Are you getting a light touch? Are you holding the body, arm, wrist, and paper in positions that will encourage a light, elastic movement? Does your wrist move as the pen moves? Do you grip the pen? Does your writing show ease, or does it look cramped? Are your down strokes as light as the up strokes? Are you practicing regularly and faithfully, or spasmodically and impatiently. Are you working, or do you live in hope with your arms folded. Success smiles on those who roll up their sleeves and go to work with a purpose. You can't dream yourself into being a penman.

LESSON 11.

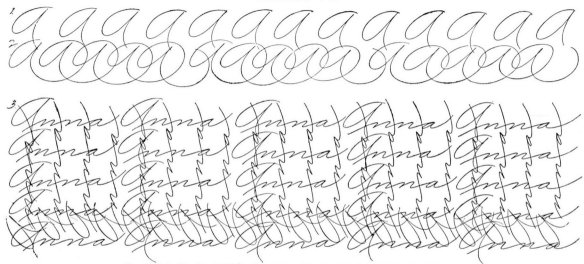

No. 1, 60 to 70.   No. 2, 10 to 12 groups.   No. 3, entire exercise in about 3 minutes.

Direct motion exercises.

Begin this lesson with practice on movement drill in Lessons 2 and 24. Make many lines of the "A" singly, then **join** in groups of five without lifting the pen, as shown in copy No. 2. This is **a** very fine movement exercise and should **be** practiced a little daily until thoroughly mastered. When one attains sufficient movement to enable him to make this exercise with absolute ease and freedom, he has sufficient m vement for all practical purposes. These letters and exercises cannot be satisfactorily done if there is the least tightness or cramping of the muscles and joints. Lay down the **pen** frequently and drop the arm by the side, allowing it to hang perfectly loose and limp. This produces relaxation.

No. 3—Fill the line with 5 words and make in groups of 5 lines, skipping a line between groups. Cross write as shown. **Time** yourself on speed. Keep lines light and make the page neat looking. Compare slant occasionally with slant chart on page 14.

Finish the "A" below the line with a vanishing hair line. Don't bring it more than half way to the line below.

—26—

LESSON 12.

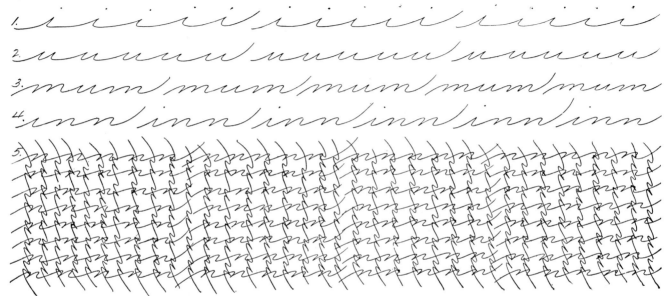

No. 1, 10 to 12 groups, dotted. No. 2, 16 to 20 groups. No. 3, 20. No. 4, 16 to 20, dotted. No. 5, about 5 minutes.

    This is largely a review on lateral motion given in Lessons 3 and 4, and it is desired that you keep in mind the necessity of looseness of the elbow joint. **Looseness, freedom** and **relaxation** are absolutely essential for executing this work in a satisfactory manner.

    Note the number of groups and lines in these copies and make the same on your paper. Make all in groups of 5 lines and if desired you may cross write as in No. 5. The small n's consist of 8 lines as you will notice which are crossed. Write a line between each ruled line on your paper and in crossing these lines space them about the same, although do not rule lines for the crossing. Use your eye for this spacing, endeavoring to get the lines spaced about the same as the horizontal lines. Read "Dots and Periods," Lesson 10, and apply to the dotting of the "i's."

—27—

LESSON 13.

No. 1—Entire exercise in about 2 minutes. No. 2, 14 to 16 words per minute.

Exercises on **Direct motion.**

No. 1—Make a full page, 10 letters to the line. Don't shade the down strokes; retrace the up stroke with the last down stroke, part way.

Turn the sheet around and write cross ways as shown. This copy may be used in groups, or not, as desired.

No. 2—Write group after group, 4 words to the line. Fill the line. Keep words directly under each other. **Make light lines.**

DON'T GET DISCOURAGED.

We all experience days, in penmanship practice as well as in other things, when everything seems to go wrong. You may not be able to write as well today as yesterday. You may feel like giving up. Don't tolerate the thought; tomorrow, or next day, you will feel ashamed of today's discouragement. No one can practice earnestly and studiously without improving. Don't try to judge your improvement by comparing the writing done yesterday with that of today. Improvement doesn't show so quickly. Judge rather by weeks and months. If you are writing with greater ease and freedom, with lighter touch, you're improving, even though the letters may be worse than before.

Good penmanship requires time and effort. It wouldn't be worth much if it could be had in a day. Everybody would have it then.

One might as well try to dip the Atlantic dry with a spoon as to imagine he can obtain knowledge, and skill, and high position and yet be rocked in the lap of luxury and ease.

Write a specimen every week or every month, place in an envelope, seal, lay away and don't open until a week or a month later.

LESSON 14.

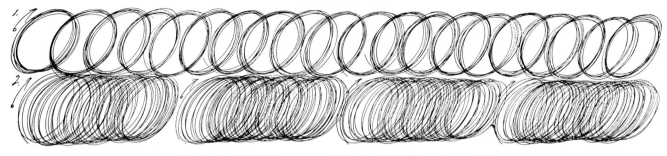

No. 1. about 15 10 times around. No. 2 150 to 200 ovals per minute.

Indirect Movement Drills.

This lesson begins the indirect, or inverted motion. Note the direction of the arrow—up on the left and down on the right.

No. 1—Make two spaces high and retrace each oval 6 to 10 times, rapidly. Overlap as shown.

No. 2—Running oval, two spaces high, and very compact. Make as rapidly as speed indicated, and down strokes **very light.**

These will be found difficult after having devoted so much practice to the direct oval, hence, don't become discouraged, because you can't make them as well as the other ovals. Hereafter, practice both the direct and indirect exercises during the same practice period.

STRENGTH AND DASH.

All writing shows plainly how it was executed. The weak, wabbly, and zigzag lines were made slowly, even may have been **drawn,** instead of **written.** The smooth, clean-cut, inspiring lines were made with considerable speed. Occasionally some one has nerves steady enough to finger (or draw) a smooth line slowly, but they are few and far between; and even then their writing is impractical for want of speed. There is little place in the business world of today for the slow, exceedingly painstaking writer.

Put life and vigor into your writing by pushing the pen with strength and boldness. Do this and your lines will show it; the writing will look more business-like, even if there are inaccuracies in form. Cultivate a regular, measured speed; such as will enable you to maintain fair control of the hand. Don't tolerate irregular and jerky motion. Don't begin a **word** slowly and increase speed until by the time the last letter is reached the hand is running away with the pen.

LESSON 15.

No. 1, 8 to 9, 10 times up and down, 10 times around. No. 2, 10, 15 times up and down. No. 3, 40 to 50. No. 4, 10 groups. No. 5, 15 words.

Indirect motion exercises.

No. 1—Make about 10 up and down strokes and encircle with oval retraced 6 to 10 times, without lifting the pen. Note the direction by the arrow. Don't put any pressure on the pen.

No. 2—The straight line movement drill finished with B. Four to the line.

No. 3—Make in groups of 5 lines, 13 letters to the line, leaving a blank line between groups. Bring the finish well up into the last oval. Large loop in connecting the two ovals. (See Form explanation Lesson 52.)

No. 4—Three groups of 5 letters each to the line and in groups of 5 lines.

No. 5—Four words to the line and in groups of 5 lines. Don't allow the pen to be lifted until the word is completed.

SPEED.

Watch your speed by timing yourself occasionally and noting the difference in your speed and that indicated beneath the copies. Notice that the faster you make a capital the smoother it is. The same is largely true of small letters, but hardly so much speed and dash can be used on them without greatly sacrificing the form. If you covet a good handwriting don't indulge in a slow, snail-like motion. You can't get it that way.

LESSON 16.

No. 1 about 2½ lines a minute. No. 2 40 to 50. No. 3, about 20 words per minute.

Indirect motion exercises. Note speed indicated for each.

No. 1—Begin with a small loop. This loop is important, since eleven capitals have the loop beginning. Realize that it must be learned (unless the dot or **fish-hook** beginning is preferred) and go at it with determination.

Make the movement drill and letter alternately. (See form explanation Lesson 63.) Keep the movement all the time. Make the arm swing easily, and **do not shade—make light lines.** Finish below the line with a vanishing hair line.

No. 2—Make a whole page of the "M," 11 to the line, 5 lines to a group, and as nearly the speed indicated as possible.

No. 3—Make a whole page of "Mum," 6 to the line and 5 lines to a group.

HOW IS YOUR MOVEMENT.

Are you compromising between finger and muscular movement; endeavoring to get muscular movement, but loathe to give up finger movement? You may feel that you cannot form letters well with muscular movement; therefore, in order to write more accurately you resort to the use of the fingers. If this is the case you must either quit it, else continue to write a poor hand. Resign yourself to free movement, no matter how you form the letters. You can soon control your movement if you are determined, and will practice studiously and with daily regularity.

CONCENTRATE YOUR MIND.

Practicing to "kill time" won't accomplish much. If you want the best results keep your whole attention on the work while at it. Don't permit the mind to wander into other channels. Fifteen minutes' practice when one feels in the mood **and with the mind concentrated,** will accomplish more than an hour of listless practice.

LESSON 17.

[handwriting practice: rows of O and N letters, "Naming Naming Naming Naming", "Nine men mining in an iron mine."]

No. 1, about 2½ lines a minute. No. 2, 50 to 60. No. 3, about 12 to 14 words. No. 4 3 lines per minute.

Begin the lesson with practice on drills Nos. 1 and 2, Lesson No. 144—Begin with small loop, same as "M" in Lesson 14. Retrace the oval exercises and letter alternately. (Form explanation lesson 64.)

No. 2—Twelve letters to the line and group after group, even pages of it. Keep the arm swinging easily. Don't begin to cramp and tension the muscles and joints. **Lines light and unshaded.**

No. 3—Fill the line with four words. Keep on the line, letters uniform in height and spacing.

No. 4—Fill the entire line with this sentence. Make in groups of 5 lines. Maintain an easy, swinging motion. See Lesson 18, below, and follow instructions as to spacing of words.

LESSON 18.

[handwriting practice: "men mining", "Many men mining in a mine."]

SPACING OF WORDS IN SENTENCES

The appearance of writing, especially in a written letter or any kind of body writing, depends quite largely upon the spacing between words. Some leave entirely too much space between them, while others crowd them too close together. The most appropriate rule and in every way the best for this, is to begin the following word at the base of an imaginary perpendicular line drawn from the close of the preceding word, as illustrated above. Write many lines of the sentence, always keeping the spacing of the words in mind.

This rule for spacing applies only to words as used in forming sentences—not to separate words as used in **many** copies in the book.

—32—

LESSON 19.

No. 1—15—8 times around.   No. 2—10 to 12 Groups.   No. 3—10 to 12 words.   No. 4—3 sentences per minute.

Indirect motion exercises.

No. 1. Alternate the drill and letter, retracing the drill 6 to 10 times. Begin with the loop. (For Form see explanation Lesson 58.)

No. 2. In groups of 5 and 3 groups to the line. The first letter is begun in the usual way, but the other four have a different beginning so as to connect easily. The first letter may be made the same if desired.

No. 3. Three words to line, five lines in a group. Join the small letters to the capital without lifting pen.

No. 4. Write this copy in groups of five lines as usual. Avoid large small letters and keep the spacing of words in mind. (See Lesson 18.) Are you watching movement and touch? Also penholding? Don't become careless in making dots and periods.

No. 5—18 groups.   No. 7—20 groups per minute.

Nos. 5, 6, 7. Count five letters to the group and four groups to the line. Keep them small and note **particularly the** dot used on "c". (See explanation Lesson 31.) Bring the "e" down to the line before turning off for the next letter. (See Lesson 32.) You may also, if desired, write between the lines, and write cross-ways as well. (See Lesson 12.)

—33—

LESSON 20.

No. 1—15—8 times around.   No. 2—40 to 50.   No. 3—12 words.   No. 4—3 lines per minute.

A continuation of **indirect** motion exercises. Begin with practice on Copy 1, Lesson 15, and Supplemental Exercises, page 75.

No. 1. Begin with small loop (see Lesson 61), and make the movement exercise and letter alternately. Keep the arm swinging freely. Don't permit any finger action in making capitals.

No. 2. Fill the line with thirteen letters and make in groups of five lines. Strokes light and rapid enough to be smooth. Time yourself by the watch. A strong, swift, swinging motion must be used if the lines are to be smooth.

Nos. 3 and 4. Fill the lines as shown. Don't allow the capitals to quite touch the line above, nor the "g's" and "y's" to touch one-space letters beneath.

RELAXATION.

Is your movement loose, or is it tight? Can you imagine how easily a well oiled ball-bearing works? This is the way the arm should roll on the pivotal muscle. To do this the elbow and shoulder joints must not bind, and the hand rests (fingers and ball of wrist) must not drag heavily. To get relaxation, **don't grip the pen**, hold it just tight enough to prevent its falling from the fingers; think more of movement than of form; and whenever you feel the arm getting tight, lay down the pen and drop the arm limp by the side; relax the muscles; then practice movement exercises a few minutes, or any easy letter exercise, before attempting difficult letters or words.

LESSON 21.

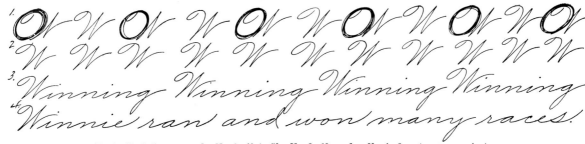

No. 1—15—8 times around. No. 2—40 to 50. No. 3—12 words. No. 4—3 sentences per minute.

Begin by practicing Copies 1 and 2, Lesson 14.

Nos. 1, 2, 3. Practice these copies in the usual way, keeping the movement and a light touch uppermost in the mind. Retrace the movement drill 6 to 10 times. (Form explanations, see Lesson 73.) Don't overlook dotting of "i's" (see Lesson 10), height of caps, and length of "g" loop.

No. 4. Fill the line as shown in copy. Keep in mind the rule for spacing words in sentences. (See Lesson 18.)

LESSON 22.

No. 1—15—8 times around. No. 2—45 to 50. No. 3—12 to 14 words per minute.

No. 1. Begin with a loop and make the movement drill and letter alternately. Retrace the drill from 6 to 10 times. Don't shade the down strokes. Finish the letter slightly below the base line with a vanishing hair line. Note that the lower loop is longest horizontally—Narrow vertically. (See form explanation, Lesson 67.)

No. 2. Make Q's 13 to the line and in groups of 5 lines, leaving a blank line between groups.

No. 3. Four words to the line and 5 lines in a group. Avoid large small letters and try to keep on the line.

LESSON 23.

No. 1—45 to 50.   No. 2—10 to 12 groups.   No. 3—14 to 16 words.   No. 4 the entire exercise, about 2½ minutes.

Practice Lessons 3 and 4 in connection.

No. 1.   (For form explanations, see Lesson 33.)   Note particularly the "dot" finish.   Four letters (w, v, b and one style of r) have this same dot finish.   Fill the line as shown.

No. 2.   Five in a group, 3 groups to the line.   Swing the pen easily; there must not be any binding.

No. 3.   Three words to the line, and in groups of 7 lines, cross-written.   Keep in mind the correct dotting of the "i." (See Lesson 10.)

No. 4.   Six words to the line and in 4 line groups, cross-written.

TOUCH.

A light touch is absolutely necessary, whether we write with a fine pen or a stub.   Ease up on the pen until the line is as fine as it will make—until the down strokes are as light as the up strokes.   Gauge the finger rests so as to support the hand, and thus allow the pen to barely skim the paper.   Don't get careless about pen-holding.   Refer to page 10 occasionally.   Don't hold the pen on the corner.

—36—

LESSON 24.

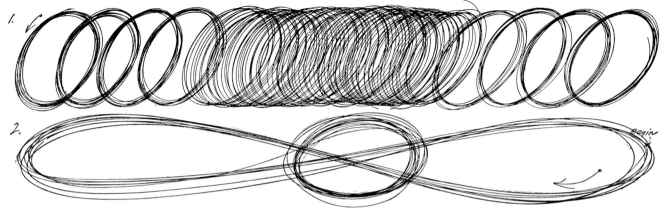

No. 1—150 to 175 revolutions. No. 2, about 4 per minute.

    No. 1. This is to be made 3 lines high (3 spaces—crossing two ruled lines on the paper). Retrace each oval about 10 times, and approximate the speed indicated.

    Large movement drills are necessary, and it is advisable to practice them a few moments in beginning every practice period. Reserve motion is necessary if one would be able to write with real ease. Just to be able to reach the extremities of capital "J" and no further, is insufficient scope. These exercises, if practiced frequently, in connection with Copy No. 2, Lesson 11, and the Supplemental Exercises (pages 73 to 80), will soon develop such a scope of motion as will enable one to reach all required points in ordinary writing with absolute ease.

    Are you giving attention to relaxation? Do you write with ease, **real** ease, or does the movement seem tight? Don't be satisfied with your movement until you have **real** ease. It can be had; "Others have it, so will I,' must be the motto.

    Never forget movement, yet as the movement becomes better established, give more and more attention to its control. The tendency of movement drill practice is to develop wildness of motion, so that, later, extra precaution becomes necessary to train the movement within the proper latitude.

"The best mirror is an old friend."

LESSON 25.

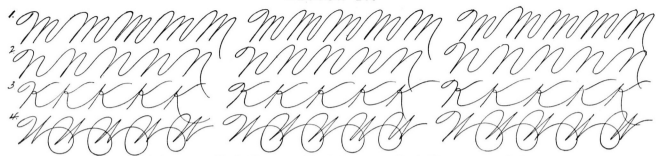

No. 1—9 groups. No. 2—12 groups. No. 3—10 groups. No. 4—10 groups per minute.

This lesson constitutes a drill in both Movement and Form. (See form explanations, Lessons 63, 64, 61, 73.) Make in groups of 5, three groups to the line. A blank line between every fifth line will add to the neatness of the page. Time your speed. Don't get discouraged because you can't make them well at first. A few minutes a day on them will bring reasonable skill within a few weeks.

LESSON 26.

No. 1—25 to 30 words. No. 2 about 30 words per minute.

(See Lesson 44 for Form explanations.)

The making of good upper loops depends principally upon the first stroke. If it is decidedly curved and not too slanting the loop can easily be finished nicely; while, on the other hand, if the first stroke is nearly straight, or if curved, yet falling over, it is utterly impossible to complete a good loop.

—38—

LESSON 27.

No. 2—45 to 50.—No. 3—15 words. No. 4—3 to 4 sentences per minute.

Practice movement drills of Lessons 14 and 15 in beginning this lesson.

No. 1. (See Lesson 59 and study explanations on Form). Begin the letter **below the** base line. Keep the **loop** narrow.

No. 2. Fill the line as in copy, 13 letters, and remember it is utterly impossible to make this letter well except **with a** strong, rolling muscular movement.

No. 3. Four words to the line, and in 5 line groups. It may be written in 7 line groups, and cross-written.

LESSON 28.

No. 2—40 to 50. No. 3—20 words. No. 4—3 sentences per minute.

Begin with movement drills, page 76. (See Lesson 60 for Form explanations.)

No. 1. Alternate with the movement drill and letter. A free, rolling motion is absolutely necessary. (Over)

—39—

No. 2. Begin **below the base line** and make the upper loop a little larger than the lower loop. **The upper part of** letter should not quite touch line above, nor the lower part touch one-space letters (m's, n's, etc.), on line beneath.

No. 3. Six words to the line and five line groups. Cross-write if desired.

No. 4. Fill the entire line with this sentence, 5 lines to the group. Notice how the four J's beginning the lines are in a column, yet do not touch, or run into each other.

LESSON 29.

ammonia ammonia ammonia

annum annum annum annum

cinnamon cinnamon cinnamon

announce announce announce

mamma mamma mamma mam

No. 1—14 to 16 words. No. 2—16 to 20. No. 3—10 to 12. No. 4—12 to 14. No. 5 about 15 words per minute.

This lesson may be used in connection with practice on nearly all of the preceding lessons. Such words are excellent practice, both for movement and for acquiring control of the movement. An earnest effort should be made to form the letters as accurately as your skill will permit. Notice particularly the connective lines and get the m's and n's round on top turns. Space the lines evenly, and keep as nearly on the line as you can. Avoid large letters and get them to line on top as well as at the bottom.

It is suggested that No. 1 be written in groups of eight lines, and cross-written; No. 2 in groups of six lines, No. 3, nine lines; No. 4, nine lines, and No. 5, six lines, all cross-written. A blank line might better be left between each of the groups so as to present a neater appearance.

Keep the hand turned well to the left, so as to push the pen ahead of the hand rather than to pull it after the hand, as is the case when the hand is thrown far to the right, with the wrist on the edge. Watch your position frequently and keep the paper in such position that the pen will touch both ends of the same line when swinging the hand back and forth across the page. Hold the pen loosely, just tight enough to keep it from falling from the fingers. Relax the joints and muscles so that all these words may be written with the greatest possible ease. If you would improve rapidly you must have daily practice, and keep reviewing the preceding lessons.

"Let others laud thy praises.'

—40—

LESSON 30.

Round turns
Sharp & retraced.

All round turns
Down strokes same slant.
sharp-retraced

Sharp & retraced.
Round turns

n's—50 to 60.   m's—45 to 55.   u's—55 to 65.   Words, 3 to 4 lines per minute.

Because you are beginning Part III, don't imagine you have finished Part II. Some part of the preceding lessons should be reviewed every day.

This method of presenting Form, by directing attention to the important points—the "boiled down" instructions attached to the letter, a constant reminder, commends itself at once as impressive, and a practical way of teaching Form.

PLAN OF PRACTICE.
(To be used for Lessons 30 to 50.)

Make 5 lines of each letter separately, beginning at the top of the page; leave a blank line and follow with 5 lines of the letter connected in groups of 5, three groups to the line. Finish the page with groups of the word, making the same number on the line as shown in the copy. **The words may be cross-written if desired.**

Keep a strong, loose, swinging motion, but begin to put forth special effort to control the movement. The foregoing copies and exercises in Part II have had a strong tendency to develop a wild carelessness, which must be overcome, and this is a good time to begin the process of "taming it." **For Form, refer frequently to pages 73 and 74.**

FIGURES.

It is suggested that figure practice be taken up now and the last few minutes of each practice period be devoted to them. (See Lessons 47, 48, 49 and 50, pages 50 and 51.) Turn to these and practice them daily.

—41—

LESSON 31.

Don't make a hook here.
Don't lift pen here.
Bring to line before turning up.
Slim oval.

a a a a aaaaa aaaaa

manna manna manna man

Don't lift pen here.
Dot - not a loop.

c c c c cccc ccccc

cannon cannon cannon cannon

Don't lift pen
Close, but don't make a loop.
Egg shaped—
Rounder than "a"

o o o o ooooo o o oo

ounce ounce ounce ounce ounce

a's—50 to 60. c's and o's—60 to 70. Words, 3 to 4 lines per minute.

Begin this and all the following lessons with from 5 to 10 minutes on one or more movement drills. Begin on the top line and make 5 lines of single "a's," 13 to a line, then 5 lines of "a's" connected, 5 letters in a group and 3 groups to the line. Then finish the page with "manna," making it in groups, and cross-writing if desired. Practice the "c" and "o" in the same way. That will be three pages of writing in this lesson, besides the figures. The initiatory stroke may be omitted from each of these letters if desired.

LESSON 32.

Leave open.
Round turn.
Bring to line before turning up.

e e e e eeeee eeeee

amen amen amen amen amen

Round turn
Round turn
Begin on line & make upward

x x x x xxxxx xxxxx

maxim maxim maxim maxim

e's—70 to 80. x's—45 to 55. Words, 3 to 4 lines a minute.

Study the forms and instructions carefully. Practice in the same way as instructed for Lesson 31, above. Note the "x." Cross it and dot the "i" after the word is written. Don't stop in the middle of the word to do either.

LESSON 33.

Sharp: a dot – not a line.
straight line.
Round turn.

i i i i i i i i i i i i i

inman inman inman inman

Sharp points Dot. Leave open.
Round turns.

w w w w w w w w w w

winnow winnow winnow win

Round turn. Dot.
Round turn.

v v v v v v v v v v v v

venom venom venom venom

i's—55 to 65. w's—45 to 55. v's—55 to 65. Word copies, 3 to 4 lines per minute.

Follow the same plan of practice suggested for Lesson 31. Keep the movement free and make lines light. Do not shade down strokes, except the little dot finish on "w" and "v." Figure practice.

LESSON 34.

Don't lift pen here.
Retrace to here.
Straight line.
Slim oval – like "a"

d d d d ddddd ddddd

dinner dinner dinner dinner d

Cross short – horizontal.
Don't lift pen.
Retrace to here.
Round turn.

t t t t t t ttttt ttttt

tinner tinner tinner tinner t

d's—50 to 60. t's—40 to 50. Word copies, 3 lines per minute.

Practice the same as lessons just preceding. These two letters are twice as high as "a." The initiatory stroke of "d" may be omitted if desired. Make the "t" cross **short and horizontal**. It should be midway between the top of the letter and the top of "i" and other one-space letters.

—43—

LESSON 35.

This much higher than 'm'
Oval shoulder not sharp
Bring well to line before turning.
Dot—retrace up stroke—
Retrace part way up.

r's—55 to 65. Words, 3 to 4 lines per minute.

This is considered a difficult letter. If you have trouble with it, resolve to devote 10 minutes a day to it, regularly, until you can make it well. You will soon get it. As you practice it you will occasionally make a good one, then after a time, you will make good ones more frequently. Watch closely and soon you will catch the motion, or twist, with which it is done, and your trouble with it is largely over.

Notice the "r" used in finishing "murmur." This should never be used except in ending words. Figure practice.

LESSON 36.

This much higher than 'm'
Well rounded curve.
Close here – don't loop.

s's—45 to 55 words, 3 to 4 lines per minute.

It is advised that you follow the same plan of practice for this difficult letter as suggested for the "r" above. Make the down stroke well rounded and close (connect) at bottom. Follow same plan of practice and arrangement as preceding lessons. Don't forget figure practice.

"Every cloud has a silver lining."

LESSON 37.

small oval
close here but don't loop.
short, narrow loop.

p p p p p p p ppppp ppppp

penman penny puny pantomime

Don't lift pen
Slim—like a:
Join on blue line.
Short and narrow loop

q q q q q q q qqqqq qqqqq

quinine quince quart quarry quit.

p's—45 to 55.   g's—45 to 55.   Words, 3 to 4 lines per minute.

Study the letters closely. Get a clear and correct conception of the forms. You can't hope to make a good letter before you know how it is made. It must be in the head before it can be put on paper.

Practice the letters separately and connected. Make them, also the words, in groups. Figure practice.

LESSON 38.

Round turn
Sharp & retraced.
cross on the line—
Round
Loop narrow and short.

y y y y y y y y y y y

yyyyy yyyyy yyyyy

young young young young

y's—50 to 60 and words 3 to 4 lines per minute.

Practice same as instructed for preceding lessons. Make the first turn at top **round**, the loop **short, narrow** and finish by crossing on the line. Do not bring the loop low enough to touch one space letters on line beneath. Make the loop with a free swing, and use a little finger action to help out, if desired. Figure practice should not be overlooked.

"Hope deferred maketh the heart sick.

—45—

LESSON 39.

A dot — not a line.

Sharp.

Cross on the line.
Loop short and narrow.

j's—40 to 50. Words, 3 to 4 lines per minute.

Study the letter and instructions attached. Get a clear, and correct conception of it, then criticise the letters as you make them. As you see an error, endeavor to correct it in following letters.

Practice in the same way as preceding lessons. Begin with a few minutes on movement drills, then fill a page, or more, with these copies as usual. Figure practice.

LESSON 40.

Slim like "a".

Don't lift pen, and don't hook nor loop this turn.

Cross on line, finish above the line.

Narrow.

Short loop.

g's—50 to 60. Words, 3 to 4 lines per minute.

The initiatory stroke may be omitted when the letter begins a word, if desired.

Practice in the usual way, beginning with movement drills, ovals, straight lines, etc., then practice Copy No. 4, Lesson 3, and finish with a page or more of the above.

Make the "g's" with a free swing, assisted with a little finger action. Loop short, narrow and crossed on the line. The "g" when ending a word may be dropped straight like the stem of figure 9. This is an appropriate figure to practice with this lesson.

"He prayeth best who loveth best."

—46—

LESSON 41.

Round turn.
Not a loop
Loop short & narrow.

z's—50 to 60. **Words 3 to 4 lines per minute.**

This may be classed as another difficult letter. Practice it in the same way as recommended for "r" and "s," (Lessons 35 and 36). **Do not loop it, but retrace.** Almost pure muscular movement should be used for all lower loops, although slight finger action is not objectionable. Practice in the usual way, and remember figure practice.

It is not expected that everyone will get the exact speed indicated, but all should try to approximate it.

LESSON 42.

Well curved
Round turn - not sharp.
Straight line all the way down except the round turns at top and bottom.
Oval turn - not very round.

l's—55 to 60. **Words, 3 to 4 lines per minute.**

This lesson begins the upper loops. These, too, are not real easy, yet if you will just remember that the **first stroke** is the **most important** one, you will avoid much trouble. The first stroke must be **thoroughly curved**, and **standing pretty straight** (not falling over). When so made the back, or down stroke, comes more naturally in place.

Study the letter and attached instructions, and practice in the usual way (see Lesson 30). In addition, make a 5-line group of the "l" exercise with the straight lines between, also remember figures.

—47—

LESSON 43.

Well curved | *Loop same as "l & b"*
Same as small "n"
Sharp & retraced

h h h h h hɪɪɪɪɪɪh hɪɪɪɪɪɪh
hhhhh hhhhh hhhhh hhhhh hhh
humming hulling hulling hulling

h's—50 to 60. Words about 3 lines per minute.

The stem or loop is similar to the "l" (Lesson 42), and the finish same as "n" (Lesson 30).

Use combined movement for all upper loops. The fingers should push and pull some to assist the muscular motion. Many **claim** to make loops, both upper and lower, with pure muscular movement, although the few **really do it.**

Practice in the usual way (see Lesson 30). Also make a 5-line group of the exercise, embodying the straight lines, or "push and pull" drill. Figure practice.

LESSON 44.

Well curved | *Round turn - not sharp*
Back straight - same as "l"
Leave open here
Retraced dot
Round

b b b b b b bɪɪɪɪɪb bɪɪɪɪɪb
bbbbb bbbbb bbbbb bbbbb bbbbb
bub bub bub bub bub bub bub
bubble bubble bubble bubble bub

b's—50 to 60. Words about 3 lines per minute.

The loop is same as "l" (Lesson 42) and the finish like "w" and "v" (Lessons 23 and 33). Read the instructions for these lessons and apply them here. Some finger action will probably assist.

Practice in the usual manner (see Lesson 30), and make a 5-line group of the movement drill. Remember **figure practice.**

—48—

LESSON 45.

Curve up stroke thoroughly and stand it fairly straight.
Open space here.
small & narrow loop.
straight line.
Retrace

k k k k k kkkkk kink
kkkkk kkkkk kkkkk kkkkk
kink kink kink kink kink k

k's—40 to 50. Words about 3 lines per minute.

The loop is the same as "h" loop (Lesson 43). Study the last part very closely. It isn't easy to make, hence **be** sure you know how you are trying to make it. (Style under "Optional Forms," page 13, may be used, if preferred.)

Keep your freedom of movement all the time. Don't deceive yourself into believing you are using a free movement, if there is any sensation of cramping or binding anywhere in the hand **or arm**. Practice in the usual way. (See Lesson 30).

LESSON 46.

Cross here.
Curve up stroke thoroughly and stand it fairly straight.
Back absolutely straight except short turns at top and bottom.
connect at blue line on on the paper - the base line.
Narrow loop.

f f f f f f f f f f f
fffff fffff fffff fffff fffff
full full full full full full full full

f's—40 to 50. Words about 3 lines per minute.

This is the longest small letter in the alphabet. In all your study of the letter and instructions attached, **keep** this uppermost in your mind—**the back is straight** except the very short turns at top and bottom. Connect the **lower** loop to the stem **at the base line.**

Fill the page in the usual way, and conclude your practice period with figures.

"One man's pleasure is another man's pain."

—49—

LESSON 47.

Short straight line - unshaded

Short line · Slight curve.
Bottom horizontal.
stop on line -

Dot or fish hook beginning.
·Horizontal.

Stem comes below line.

/ /

4 4 4 4 4 4 4 4 4 4 4 4 4 4 4 4 4 4

4 4 4 4 4 4 4 4 4 4 4 4 4 4 4 4 4 4

7 7 7 7 7 7 7 7 7 7 7 7 7 7 7 7 7 7 7

7 7 7 7 7 7 7 7 7 7 7 7 7 7 7 7 7 7 7

1's—120; 4's—60 to 70; 7's—75 to 80 per minute.

Study these figures closely, getting a correct mental picture of them. The "1" is a short, straight, **unshaded** line. The bottom of "4" is **horizontal** (parallel with line on the paper) and should be down very close to the line. The bottom extends far to the right, **beyond the cross** made by the last stroke. Don't bring the last stroke below the base line. **The** top of "7" is also **horizontal** (not oblique) and the stem is brought below the base line. Only two figures extend **below** the line, "7" and "9." All others **rest on the line.**

Practice all in 5 line groups, with a vacant line between. **Do not shade any part of any figure.**

LESSON 48.

Fish hook start.
Come straight to the line.

Fish hook start.
Pull straight down.
Don't loop.
Larger than top

Very short
stem
Loop & finish well to left
Cross short and horizontal.
Broad shoulders.

Large oval finished well to left

2 2 2 2 2 2 2 2 2 2 2 2 2 2 2 2 2

3 3 3 3 3 3 3 3 3 3 3 3 3 3 3 3 3 3 3

3 3 3 3 3 3 3 3 3 3 3 3 3 3 3 3 3 3

5 5 5 5 5 5 5 5 5 5 5 5 5 5 5 5 5 5

5 5 5 5 5 5 5 5 5 5 5 5 5 5 5 5 5 5

2's—80 to 100; 3's—60 to 70; 5's—60 to 70 per minute.

Begin "2" and "3" with a fish-hook or dot. A loop beginning will tend toward too large figures. The "2" may be looped at the bottom if desired, instead of the finish shown. The "5" is usually begun with the stem; the cross (short horizontal line) being made last. **Join the cross to the stem.**

Practice in 5 line groups, and cross-write if desired. **No shade anywhere.**

"A man's destiny is always dark."

—50—

LESSON 49

Connect.
Egg shaped.
Connect
Slim-like "a"
Just above line
slight curve
Small loop
Bring well down
Begin here
Gradual curve.
Narrow.

0 0 0 0 0 0 0 0 0 0 0 0 0 0 0 0 0 0 0 0 0 0 0 0 0 0 0

9 9 9 9 9 9 9 9 9 9 9 9 9 9 9 9 9 9 9 9 9 9 9 9 9 9 9

6 6 6 6 6 6 6 6 6 6 6 6 6 6 6 6 6 6 6 6 6 6 6 6 6 6

6 6 6 6 6 6 6 6 6 6 6 6 6 6 6 6 6 6 6 6 6 6 6 6 6

8 8 8 8 8 8 8 8 8 8 8 8 8 8 8 8 8 8 8 8 8 8 8 8

8 8 8 8 8 8 8 8 8 8 8 8 8 8 8 8 8 8 8 8 8 8 8 8

0's—100; 9's—80 to 90; 6's—60 to 70; 8's—60 to 70 per minute.

Study these figures and instructions attached. Be sure you know how they should be made, and criticise your figures severely. **Make all figures small, and do not shade any part of any figure.**

Notice where "8" is begun, that the crooked line is made first. It can be well made in the opposite direction, and there is no serious objection to that habit. Practice in 5-line groups, and cross-write if desired.

LESSON 50.

1 2 3 4 5 6 7 8 9 0 1 2 3 4 5 6 7 8 9 0 1

2 3 4 5 6 7 8 9 0 1 2 3 4 5 6 7 8 9 0 1 2

3 4 5 6 7 8 9 0 1 2 3 4 5 6 7 8 9 0 1 2 3

4 5 6 7 8 9 0 1 2 3 4 5 6 7 8 9 0 1 2 3 4

5 6 7 8 9 0 1 2 3 4 5 6 7 8 9 0 1 2 3 4 5

$ $ $ $ $ $ c/o c/o c/o a/c a/c a/c c/o c/o c/o @ @ @

$97⁵⁰ $97⁵⁰ $97⁵⁰ $97⁵⁰ $97⁵⁰ $97⁵⁰

$3 295²⁵ $3 295²⁵ $3 295²⁵ $3 295²⁵   325²⁵

Note the arrangement. By making them in blocks, either consecutively, as above, or miscellaneously, they can be counted quickly. Work for a speed of from 100 to 125 good figures per minute. Make in 10-line groups instead of 5 lines, as shown.

LESSON 51.

Slim — *Nearly closed*
Retraced
Finish below line with vanishing hair line.

𝒜 𝒜 𝒜 𝒜 𝒜 𝒜 𝒜 𝒜

Ammon Ammon Ammon Ammon

Annie ran across the grassy lawn.

A's—50 to 60. Words and sentences 3 to 4 lines per minute.

Begin this lesson with a few minutes' practice on Lesson 5. Practice the single letter in 5-line groups, making 13 letters to the line. Practice the word "Ammon" in 5 line groups also, 4 words to the line. Finish the page with 5 line groups of the sentence. Be careful that the capitals do not quite touch the line above nor the lower loops touch the letters on the line beneath. Continue daily figure practice.

LESSON 52.

Well rounded
Large loop.
Retrace.
Finish in here.

ℬ ℬ ℬ ℬ ℬ ℬ ℬ ℬ ℬ ℬ

Banner Banner Banner Banner ℬ

Become a good penman; it will pay.

B's—45 to 55. Words and sentences, 3 to 4 lines per minute.

Begin this lesson with a few minutes' practice on Lesson 15. Be sure you have a correct mental picture of the letter. Practice in the usual way, making the 5 line groups of the single letter, 13 to a line, then a group of "Banner," and finish the page with 5 line groups of the sentence, leaving a blank line between groups.

—52—

LESSON 53

Open space
Good sized loop
Back well rounded.
Round.
Begin above line.

Round.
Narrow loop.
Up stroke thoroughly curved
Small loop.
Finish brought well down.

C C C C CCCCC

Common Common Cannon Cannon

Commoners in a common community.

C's—50 to 60. Words and sentences, 3 to 4 lines per minute.

Use the style "C" you prefer, but when you have made your selection, stick to it. Be sure you are using an **easy,** rolling motion. Practice Lesson 7 in connection.

LESSON 54.

Compound curve.
Enclose end of stem.
Small
Stand back about vertical.
Rest on line.

D D D D D D DDDDD

Denman Denman Denman Denman

Due Daniel D Denman on Demand

D's—40 to 50. Words and sentences, 3 to 4 lines per minute.

Practice Lesson 8 in connection. Notice especially that both the **stem** and the **oval rest** on the line, neither **above** nor **below.** Are you writing with ease and freedom and are your lines absolutely light, without any shade or pressure on the down strokes? Practice in groups as usual. Thirteen single letters, 3 groups of connected letters and **four words to a line.**

—53—

LESSON 55.

well rounded
Dot, fish hook or small loop.
Bring loop well to the right.
Small loop
Open space

𝓔 𝓔 𝓔 𝓔 𝓔 𝓔 𝓔 𝓔𝓔𝓔𝓔

Emmons Eminence Emmons Eminence

Eminence is not gained by indolence

E's—45 to 50. Words and sentences, 3 to 4 lines per minute.

Letter "E" is considered difficult, but can be quickly mastered if studied carefully, and practiced earnestly. Be a severe critic of all your work, and keep movement well in mind. Your letters can not be well made with a cramped movement. Practice the single letter, 13 to a line; 3 groups of the connected letters, 5 letters in a group; and four words to a line. Figure practice.

LESSON 56.

Large loop.
Flat or Drooped
open space
Don't touch
Compound curve
Keep close to the stem.
Horizontal
Well rounded

𝓕 𝓕 𝓕 𝓕 𝓕 𝓕 𝓕

Famine Famine Famine Famine

Free movement must be acquired 𝓕

F's—35 to 40. Words and sentences, 3 to 4 lines per minute.

Study the letter and instructions carefully. Practice the single letter in 5 line groups, 13 letters to the line; the words 4 to the line and in 5 line groups. Finish the page with 5 line groups of the sentence. Make the stem first and the top last. The cross is made before the top, and without lifting the pen.

—54—

LESSON 57.

Gammon Gammon Gammon Gunner

Good penmanship pays big dividends.

G's—40 to 50. Words and sentences, 3 to 4 lines per minute.

Practice supplemental exercise page 76 in connection. Study the letter and instructions until you have a clear conception of a correct "G." Practice the single letter in 5 line groups, 13 letters to the line, and the connected letters in groups of 5, 3 groups to the line. Practice the words and sentences as usual. Figure practice.

LESSON 58.

Hammond Hammond Hammond Hum

Hammond is a man's name. Hammond.

H's—40 to 45. Words and sentences, 3 to 4 lines per minute.

Study the letter as usual and practice Lesson 19 in beginning. Make the single letter 13 to the line, and the connected letters in groups of 5 and 3 groups on a line. Practice the word and sentence as usual.

—55—

LESSON 59.

Narrow---
Horizontal
Full curve and
slant it pretty
straight up and
down

Round   Begin below line.

Inning Inning Inning Inning

I am gaining in my penmanship

I's—40 to 50. Words and setences, 3 to 4 lines per minute.

Study the letter and instructions and practice Lesson 27 in connection. Make 13 single letters to the line and in 5 line groups. Make the connected letters in groups of 5 and 3 groups to the line. Practice the word and sentences in groups, and fill the entire line with the 4 words, and with the sentence, as shown.

LESSON 60.

Full
curve
Back straight
except short
turns at top
and bottom.
cross
on line
Begin below
Narrower than
upper loop.

January January January Junior

January and July each have 31 days.

J's—40 to 50. Words and sentences, 3 to 4 lines per minute.

Study this letter and instructions. Notice particularly that the upper loop is larger than the lower and that the back is practically straight. Compare your slant now and then with Slant Chart, page 14. Practice Lesson 28 and Supplemental Exercise, page 76, in connection. Make 15 single letters to the line in 5 line groups, and the connected letters in groups of 5, 3 groups to the line. Practice words and sentence, as usual. Figure practice.

LESSON 61.

Open space.
Compound curve.
Loop
Small loop touching the stem.
Compound curve.

Stop firm *Finish below. Raise pen while in motion*

Kinney Kinney Kinney Kinney Kinney

Kinky lines are caused by slow motion.

K's—40 to 50. Words and sentences, 3 to 4 lines per minute.

Practice Lesson 20, and Copy 3, Lesson 25, in connection. Make the single letter 13 to the line and in 5 line groups, and the connected letters in groups of 5 letters, 3 groups to a line. Practice the word and sentence in 5 line groups.

LESSON 62.

Begin above line. *Narrow loop.*
Full curve.
Compound curve.
Round turn
Horizontal loop. *Finish below line—*

Lanning Lanning Lanning Lanning

Learn more, then you can earn more.

L's—40 to 50. Words and sentences 3 to 4 lines per minute.

Study the letter and instructions and note that the down stroke is well curved, rounded at the bottom, and that the loop is horizontal. Practice Supplemental Exercise, page 76, in connection. Make the single letter 13 to the line and in 5 line groups, and the connected letters in groups of 5, 3 groups to the line. Practice the word and sentence in 5 line groups as usual.

—57—

LESSON 63.

Open space
Round turns.
Slanting
Loop
Narrow.
Retrace part way up.
Finish below line. Raise pen while in motion so make a vanishing hair line.

M. M M M M M M M M M

Manning Manning Mammon Moon
Maude and Minnie won nine games.

M's—40 to 50. Words and sentences, 3 to 4 lines per minute.

Study the letter and instructions, noticing particularly that the parts of the letter slope downward on top. Practice Lesson 16, and Copy 1, Lesson 25, in connection. Make the single letters in groups of 5 lines, 11 letters to the line. Practice the word and sentence in the usual way, striving for smooth lines.

LESSON 64.

Open space
Round turn—not sharp.
Loop
Slanting
Retrace part way.
Finish below line Lift pen quickly.

N N N N N N N N N N N

Nannie Nannie Nannie Nannie Noun
Nannie is sewing seams on a machine.

N's—50 to 60. Words and sentences, 3 to 4 lines per minute.

Practice Lesson 17, and Copy 2, Lesson 25, in connection. Make 14 single letters to the line and in 5 line groups. Practice the word and sentence as usual in groups of 5 lines with a blank line between each group. Figure practice daily.

—58—

LESSON 65.

Egg Shaped — Connect · Small loop · Smooth lines all around. No Kinks - Make quickly

O O O O O O O O O OOOOO

Onion Onion Onion Onion Onion

O see me use muscular movement.

O's—60 to 70. Words and sentences 3 to 4 lines per minute.

Practice Lessons 5, 6 and 10 in connection. Make 13 single letters to the line and the connected letters in groups of 5, 3 groups to the line. Practice the word and sentence in 5 line groups and fill the entire lines as shown in the copies.

LESSON 66.

Well rounded not flat. · Well rounded oval. · Retrace nearly all the way up. Not looped. — Full - not flat. · Nearly all of the body to left of stem. · Just enough to enclose the stem. · Well curved. · Round turn.

P P P P P PPPPP

Panama Panama Panama Panama P

Persimmons aren't good in summertime.

P's—50 to 60. Words and sentences, 3 to 4 lines per minute.

Use either style preferred, but after the selection is made, stick to that style. Make 13 single letters to the line and the connected letters in groups of 5, 3 groups to the line. Practice the word and the sentence in the usual groups. The words in any of these lessons may be cross-written if desired. If this is done, the word "Panama" above should be written in 7 line groups to permit of a letter between lines in the cross-writing.

—59—

LESSON 67.

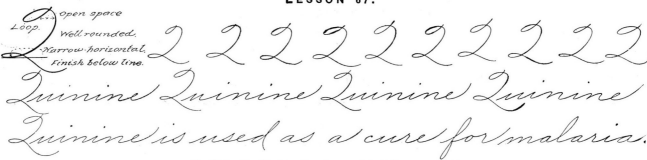

Q's—50 to 55. Words and sentences 3 to 4 lines per minute.

Study the letter and instructions and practice Lesson 22 in connection. Make 13 single letters to the line; words, 4 to the line, and practice all in groups as usual. Figure Practice.

LESSON 68.

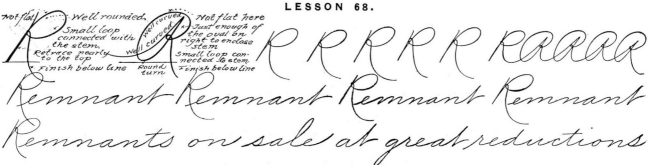

R's—45 to 55. Words and sentences 3 to 4 lines per minute.

Select either style of letter preferred. Other styles of capitals are shown on page 13 and may be used instead of the ones given, if especially desired. Make 13 single letters to the line, and the connected letters in groups of 5, 3 groups to the line. Practice the word and sentence as usual. If the word should be cross-written, write in groups of 8 lines.

LESSON 69.

S's—45 to 55. Words and sentences, 3 to 4 lines per minute.

As usual, where more than one style of letter is given, select the one desired, and stick to it. Make 13 single letters to the line, and the connected letters in **groups of 5**, 3 groups to the line. Practice the word and sentence in the usual way. Fill the lines as shown in the copies.

LESSON 70.

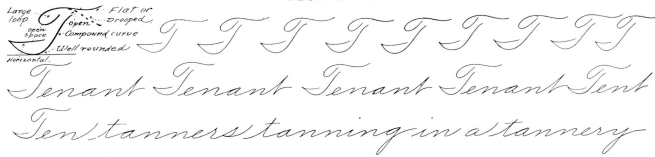

T's—45 to 55. Words and sentences, 3 to 4 lines per minute.

Study the letter closely; the stem is made first, the top last. Begin your practice on some good movement exercises. Make 13 single letters to the line, and 5 of the words. If the word is intended to be cross-written, write in **groups of 7** lines.

LESSON 71.

Open space.
About ⅓ height of first part.
Retrace about ½ way down.
Loop.
This finish if preferred.
Round. *Finish below line.*

U U U U U U U U U U

Unit Unit Unit Unit Unit Unit Unit

Use an easy muscular movement.

U's—45 to 55. Words and sentences, 3 to 4 lines per minute.

Study the letter closely with attached instructions. Make 13 single letters to the line and 5 of the words. **Practice** in groups as usual and by all means be sure that you are making light lines, and that **the small letters are low, and kept** as nearly on the line as possible.

LESSON 72.

Open space.
Loop.
About ⅔ height of first part.
Both compound curves.
Narrow—and about same width all way up
Round.

V V V V V V V V V V

Vermin Vermin Vermin Vermin Vine

Value time, it is worth money to you.

V's—55 to 65. Words and sentences, 3 to 4 lines per minute.

Study the letter and instructions attached. Begin the lesson with liberal drill on movement exercises. Make 15 **single** letters to the line and practice the word and sentence as usual. Daily figure practice.

—62—

LESSON 73.

Open Loop. Same height. Sharp & slightly retraced. About 1/3 height of other parts. Straight line. Sharp & slightly retraced.

W W W W W W W W W

Winnow Winnow Winnow Winnow Winnow, meaning to fan grain. Win.

W's—45 to 55. Words and sentences, 3 to 4 lines per minute.

Study the letter and instructions attached and practice Copy 4, Lesson 25, also movement exercises, page 75, in connection. Make 13 single letters to the line and 4 words.

LESSON 74.

Open Loop. Curved. Small loop. Bring well down.

X X X X X X X X X X

Xerxes Xerxes Xerxes Xerxes Xerxes

X is a hard letter but seldom used.

X's—40 to 50. Words and sentences, 3 to 4 lines per minute.

Study the letter and instructions attached. Make 13 single letters to the line and 5 of the words. Write in groups as usual. Don't forget figure practice.

LESSON 75.

Compound curve.
About ⅓ height of first part.
Sharp & retraced.
Finish above line.
Straight line —
Cross on line.

Open Loop.
Round.
Narrow & Short.

Y Y Y Y Y Y Y Y Y Y

Young Young Young Young Yours

Young men wanted in the army and navy.

Y's—40 to 50. Words and sentences, 3 to 4 lines per minute.

Study the letter and instructions until you are sure you know how a correct letter should be made. Practice movement exercise page 76, in connection. Make 13 single letters to the line and practice the words and sentence in the lesson as usual. Compare your slant occasionally with Slant Chart, page 14.

LESSON 76.

Rounded.
Avoid excessive curve—especially near the bottom.
Cross on line and finish above it.

Open Loop.
Small loop.
Narrow & short.

Z Z Z Z Z Z Z Z Z Z Z Z

Zimmer Zimmer Zimmer Zimmer

Zealously watch movement and form.

Z's—40 to 50. Words and sentences 3 to 4 lines per minute.

Practice movement exercises in connection, and study the letter with instructions attached. Make 14 single letters to the line and 4 of the words. Write all in groups as usual.

—64—

Sentences and Business Forms.

LESSON 77.

A good penman is always in demand.

Be sure your movement is loose and easy.

Cramped movement makes cramped writing.

Do your very best, it will be none too well.

The sentences in this and the following lessons may be practiced by themselves, or in connection with preceding Lessons, Nos. 51 to 76. These sentences are a little longer than most of those used in the preceding lessons above mentioned, and are made so purposely in order to compel smaller writing. The average student forms the habit of writing rather too large, so that some special attention and drill is necessary to make the writing smaller and more compact. It is, therefore, requested that these sentences be written small enough to go on a line, as shown in the copies. It is seldom necessary to criticise a student for small writing, therefore, little need be said to caution against it. It is suggested that these sentences be practiced in groups as advised in previous lessons.

"If you would have success, deserve It."

LESSON 78.

Every letter should be criticised by you.

Free and easy movement is very necessary.

Good figures are important. 1234567890.

Heavy touch can and must be overcome.

LESSON 79.

I'm learning to write a good business hand.

Joining words is good movement drill.

Keep the hand moving with the pen.

Looseness of movement makes smooth writing.

"In everything the golden mean is best."

LESSON 80.

Make the top of 7 and bottom of 4 horizontal.

Never give up, you can conquer if you will.

Others have become good penmen; why not I?

Practice studiously if you would improve.

LESSON 81.

Quit trifling, get down to earnest practice.

Remember movement, first, last, all the time.

See forms as they are—make them correctly.

Try to write better today than yesterday.

LESSON 82.

Utilize your spare moments; they are valuable.

Variety in practice, as in other things, is helpful.

Winning in my race for success. W

You should learn to write your name well.

LESSON 83.

F. B. Runyan.   *A. D. Putnam.*

S. D. Knapp.   *W. B. Tamblyn.*   *A. V. Lowman.*

A. H. Bowman.   *J. Sumner*

Considerable practice on signature combinations is advised. Such practice is splendid for both movement and form, and nothing is more practical than to be able to connect letters into business signatures. One point to keep in mind throughout all such practice is that the capitals should be kept as compact (close together) as possible, and yet remain plain.

"Education forms the common mind."

—68—

LESSON 84.

$417.00

Kansas City, Mo., January —

Received of Henry D. Hammond

Four hundred and seventeen dollars in

full of account.   C. R. Manning.

Receipt.

This may be practiced in pages similar to sentences. It occupies 5 lines and between each receipt a blank line may be left, so as to separate nicely.

LESSON 85.

J. H. Kemmer.   J. E. Murray.

J. W. Randall   O. M. Powers.   P. L. Hinman.

E. M. Huntsinger.   J. E. Brown.

Read the remarks concerning Lesson 83 on opposite page, and in addition to this, try to make the capitals as uniform in height as possible.

LESSON 86.

$900 00

Chicago, Ill., Feb. 24, 19

Nine months after date I promise to pay to Frank G. Smith, or order, Nine Hundred Dollars, with interest at the rate of 6% per annum. Value received.

Wm. M. Williamson.

Promissory Note.

This note occupies 6 lines and it is suggested that a blank line be left between each, if it is written a number of times on the same page.

"A good name is the best thing in the world."

LESSON 87.

Kansas City, Mo., Mar. 3, 19

At sight pay to the Commerce Trust Company of Kansas City Twenty Dollars and charge to the account of

To C. M. Johnson,
Emporia, Kans.

J. H. Brennan & Co.

Sight Draft.

This occupies 6 lines and if a number of them are written on a page, separate with a blank line between.

"A soft answer turneth away wrath."

LESSON 88.

Kansas City, Mo., May 5, 1929.

Armour Packing Co.,

City.

Gentlemen:—Should there be a vacancy in your offices for a clerk, bookkeeper, or stenographer, please consider me an applicant. Address me 510 Gloyd Bldg., or phone Ma. 2719.

Yours truly,

D. M. Kinney.

Letter of Application.

Owing to lack of space, this letter is brief, and might well be lengthened, although extreme length and unnecessary words are always to be avoided in business letters. Every one should be able to word a good letter of application as well as to be able to write it well. It acts as an introduction, and if it creates a favorable impression the applicant has a good chance for the position; whereas a poorly worded and poorly written letter would likely land in the waste basket, unanswered.

"Knowledge is gold to him who can discern."

Form Study and Supplementary Movement Exercises.

i u w m m v x a c o e r s

t d p q l h b k f g j y z

SLANT ABOUT 58°

A B C D E F G H I J K L M

N O P Q R S T U V W X Y Z

1 2 3 4 5 6 7 8 9 0

The **Base** line is the line on which writing rests, the heavy black horizontal lines above, designating the blue ruling on paper.

A **Space** in height is represented by the height of small "i"; in width by the two down strokes of small "u." The distance of a space varies with the style and size of writing.

The **Scale** in writing is three spaces above the base line, and two below, (5 spaces in all.) Only four letters fill the entire scale, small f and capitals J. Y, Z. Notice above that the Scale does not quite fill the space between two blue lines on the paper, as no letter, neither capitals nor loop, should quite touch the line above.

Classification and Relative Distance Above and Below BASE Line.

1   space above, 11 letters—i, u, w, n, m, v, x, a, c, o, e, (called 1 space letters.)
1¼ space above, 2 letters—r and s.
2   spaces above, 3 letters—t, d, p, (called semi-extended letters.)
3   spaces above, all capitals and 5 small letters—l, h, b, k, f, (called upper loop letters.)
1½ space below, 2 letters—p and q.
2   spaces below, 5 small letters—f, j, y, z, g, and 3 capitals—J, Y, Z, (lower loop letters.)

The three upper spaces of the Scale do not quite fill the space between the blue line ruling on the paper, as no letter should touch the line above, neither should any letter extend low enough to touch 1 space letters on the line beneath.

The standard of height is represented by the letter "i"; the standard of width by the letter "u."

The period and dot should be a DOT—not a line. See illustration, page 13. i and j should be dotted 2 spaces above the base line, being even with the top of t, d and p, and in line with the slant of their down stroke.

Three small letters (b, v, w) finish with a retracing, forming a sort of dot. Also one style of r finishes the same.

UPPER LOOP LETTERS. The loop itself covers 2 spaces in length, 2-3 the height of the letter. The down stroke, therefore, crosses the up stroke 1 space above Base line. The back of these loops (the down stroke) should be straight, not **humped** nor **sway-back.**

LOWER LOOP LETTERS. The loop covers 2 spaces in length, except in "p" and "q"; in these it covers 1½ space. In "f" and "q" the loop is formed by turning to the **right** at bottom turn, going upward and connecting with the down stroke at the Base line. In all others, including the three capitals, the loop is formed by turning to the **left,** at bottom turn, going upward and crossing the down stroke at the Base line.

SEMI-EXTENDED LETTERS. The "t" is crossed 1½ space above the Base line. The cross should be the same length as the width of small "u," and horizontal, (parallel with the base line.) The "d" is a small "a" with a straight line 1 space long added to the top point.

SMALL "r" AND "s." Both letters proper are 1 space high. The extra ¼ space is the point extending above.

CAPITALS. Some part of every capital extends 3 spaces above the Base line, touching the top of the Scale. The last part of M, U, V, W, Y, and the stem of F and T, is 2 spaces high. The stem, or last part of "G," is 1½ space, or half the height of the letter.

FIGURES. 1½ spaces high—all except 6, which is 2 spaces. 1 space below line—7 and 9, being the only figures that extend below the base line. The first part of 4 begins one space above, the bottom is in the middle of the space, the cross, or last part, is 1½ spaces high and stops on the base line.

It is desired that the student study carefully the chart on preceding page, and all explanations following, including those above, to the end that a clear conception of Correct Form may be learned. Correct form can't possibly be put on paper until it is first in the head. With a free, easy muscular movement, however, as the student should by this time have acquired, and with a correct conception of form, he should now be able to write a good business hand.

We feel it is only those who have not followed the instructions regarding movement up to this point who will fail.

OPTIONAL FORMS.

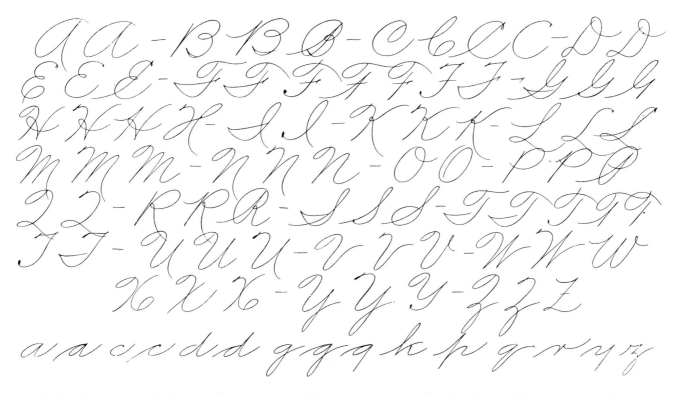

Style of letters, particularly capitals, is governed largely by taste. All of the forms above are practical, and one about as good as another. Arguments for and against can be suggested for nearly all.

SUPPLEMENTAL MOVEMENT EXERCISES.

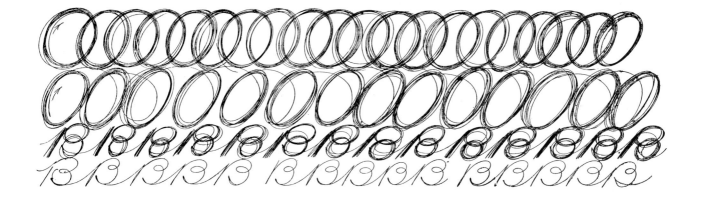
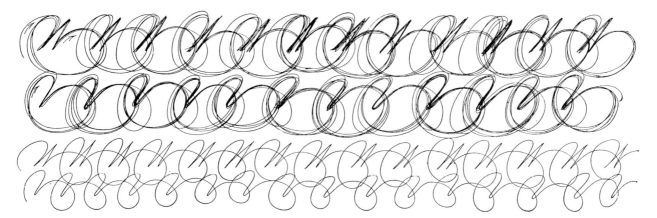

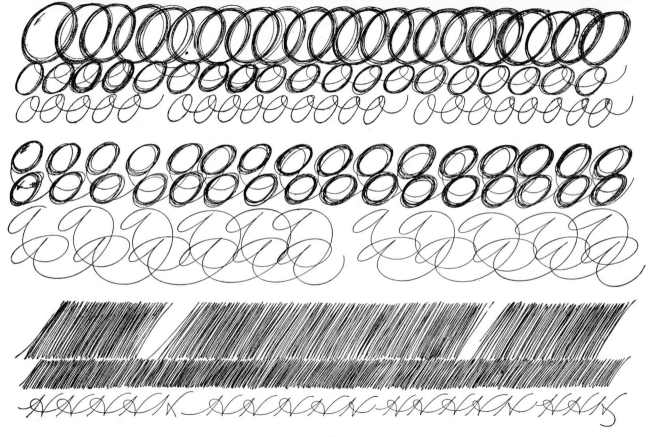

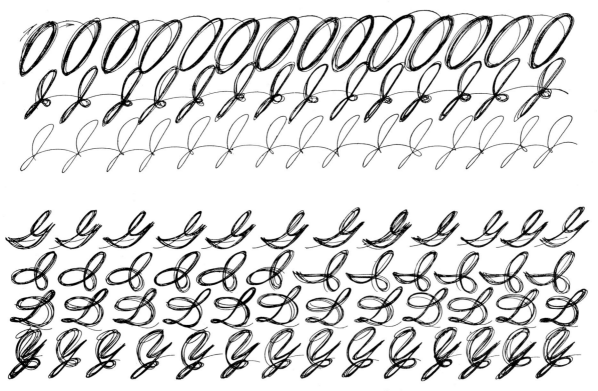

"False friends are worse than open enemies."

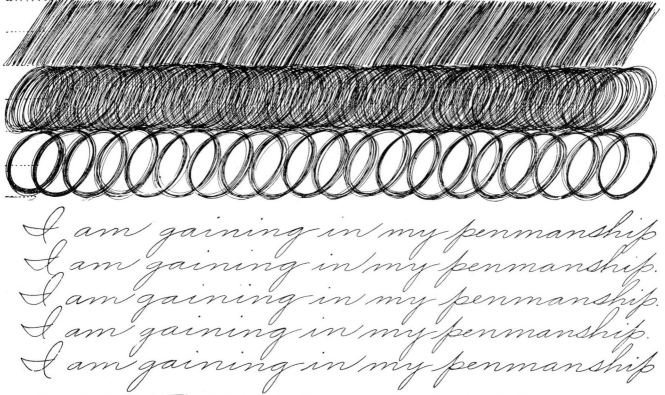

Illustrating the 5 line group method of practice. Letters and words directly under each other.
"Brain uneducated is like marble uncarved."

TAMBLYN SYSTEM TRANSPARENT FORMS.

(Business Writing)

A B C D E F G H I J K L M N

O P Q 2 R R S S T U V W X Y Z

a b c d e f g h i j k l m n o p q

r r s t u v w x y z 1 2 3 4 5 6 7 8 9 0

Compare your letters occasionally with these by placing yours directly under this transparent sheet. You can fold your sheet in order to get the particular letter you wish to compare under the copy—or you can cut your letter from your practice sheet. Don't put your sheet under until the ink is fully dry.

For greater convenience in making comparisons, we have these forms printed on a loose heavy celluloid sheet, that you can lay over your letters easily; price 20c, stamps. Order "Transparent Forms Sheet" (Business Writing.)

You can jot over your letters easily; price 30c. sample. Order "Transparent Forms Sheet." (Business Writing.)
For greater convenience in marking corrections we have these forms printed on a loose heavy celluloid sheet that

your practice sheet. Don't put your sheet under until the ink is fully dry.
your sheets in order to get the particular letter you wish to compare under the copy—so you can cut your letters from
Compare your letters occasionally with those by placing your directly under this transparent sheet. You can hold

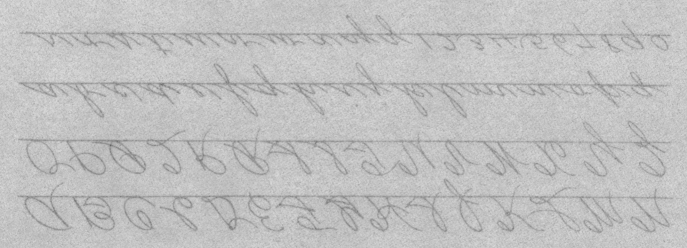

(Business Writing)
LAMBERT SYSTEM TRANSPARENT FORMS.

RTISTIC WRITING is so attractive and pleasing to the eye that it is never likely to lose its popularity. The skill displayed in its execution creates wonder and holds most people by its fascination. The fascination of artistic writing and other ornamental penmanship has started many on the road to good business writing, who otherwise might never have made the start.

One cannot hope to accomplish much in this line until a good business handwriting has first been acquired. The desire to do ornamental work tends to encourage one to put forth greater effort to acquire a good business hand, that he may then be able to master ornamental work.

After a good movement has been acquired and a business hand partly developed, practice on artistic writing is a great help to business writing by strengthening the movement.

America leads the world in ornamental penmanship. People of other countries marvel at the great number of skillful American penmen.

Our ideal is important. Low ideals mean little progress. Lofty ideals mean improvement, with a chance for the top.

CORRECT WAY TO HOLD THE PEN.

Study this illustration in connection with those on pages 7, 9 and 10. Note that the front finger and the thumb are drawn up until the joints stick out rather sharp.

The hand must not stick nor drag on the little fingers, nor the ball of the wrist. It must slide easily on these rests.

Drop the holder in the hollow between the knuckle joints of finger and thumb. Less pressure is required to make the shade when the holder is held on an angle than when held nearly vertical.

MOVEMENT.

The different movements are defined and explained on page 11. Artistic writing is done with the same movement as business writing. A bold, swinging, muscular movement for capitals, with combined movement for small letters, especially for the upper loop letters. The degree of finger movement advisable to use in making the small letters may vary with the individual, but one must be certain to keep the hand and arm working freely, so as not to fall into the use of **pure Finger** movement.

Some penmen advocate Whole Arm movement for capitals. I first learned with this movement, but am convinced that muscular movement is the proper movement, although I still use the whole arm when writing with heavy sleeves on the arm, (such as an overcoat), or when desiring to make a capital unusually large.

The large muscle of the arm can be developed to meet the requirements of all ordinary artistic writing, therefore, make up your mind to use **Muscular Movement.** Avoid tight sleeves. One loose sleeve is about all that should be kept on the arm when writing.

MATERIAL.

PAPER—Use a good quality of ruled paper. Better paper is required for shaded writing than for business writing. The pen will pick up lint on soft paper in making shades, whereas it might not in making unshaded lines in business writing.

PENS—A flexible pen must be used. The degree of fineness of point is not so essential. I recommend Tamblyn's Champion No. 5, Gillott's No. 604, or Spencerian No. 1 for beginners. Advanced students who desire finer hair lines will find **Tamblyn's Professional No. 7** or **Gillott's Principality No. 1** the best to be had.

INK—Use good black ink with a solid body, so the shades will be solid. Glossy ink is largely used, though not really necessary. There are so many makes of suitable ink on the market, that I shall not attempt to name them, although Tamblyn's Glossy Black or Eternal Black will be found good.

HOLDER—If you want the best results with least resistance, use an **oblique holder.** Shading can be done with a straight holder, but no penman now thinks of using it when an oblique can be had. There are many good holders on

the market, among them Tamblyn's 2 in 1. Get one in which the metal attachment is firm, appearing like this illustration.

ADJUSTING HOLDER.

Almost every penman adjusts his holder to suit himself, so there are almost as many ways of adjusting it as there are users, but it is generally accepted that the point of the pen should be about in line with the center of the holder when sighted down. Personally, however, I prefer the point slightly further to the right than the center. And I want it thrown over by the angle of the attachment, rather than by allowing the pen to stick out further.

It should further be so adjusted by bending the metal attachment to throw the point of the pen up or down to suit the user. Most penmen seem to like the point thrown up almost level with the top of the holder. I use mine slightly lower than this.

Then, again, the metal should be bent until the pen sets perfectly level (the eyelet dirctly on top) as you grasp the holder in your natural writing position. When properly adjusted in this respect, the pen should slide over the paper smoothly, and one should be able to make the inverted oval shade in Lesson 1, next page, and the capital "C" shade in Lesson 11, page 94, smooth and clean cut, without ragged edges. These two shades constitute my ordinary tests for holder adjustment.

POSITION.

All positions should be the same as for business writing, therefore, study very carefully all illustrations and instructions on pages 7, 8, 9 and 10 of this book.

If, however, you have the habit of holding the pen with front finger and thumb thrown out nearly straight, it will be necessary to draw them up so that the first joint of the thumb and the second joint of the front finger stick out pretty sharp. See illustration on opposite page. This enables easier pressure in making shades, and permits greater freedom of finger action when needed, as is often necessary for best results.

LESSON 1.

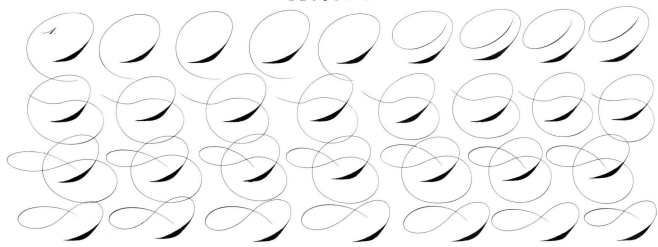

All these 30 to 35 a minute.

    This is called the **Inverted Oval** and made with indirect motion. Begin below the line in the first five on first line.
    Use a rapid swinging motion. The strokes must be bold and decisive at about the speed indicated. The shades should be made about as you would crack a whip.
    Don't fool along with a slow, snail-like motion. It won't produce results. You must make these quickly, even though poor in form. Get the speed, then improve form afterward.
    Bring the shade well down toward the line, and strive to cut it off horizontal right on the line, finishing it with a sharp point.
    Don't use any finger movement.
    In lines 2, 3, and 4 notice the curves, see how regular and clean-cut, which can be done only with a bold and rapid motion.
    Make line after line. When a page is filled lay the sheet aside and take another, then after the first is dry write crossways on the same side, and so on in that way using both sides of your paper two or three times.

LESSON 2.

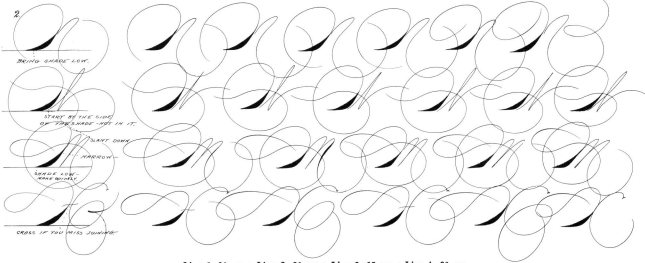

Line 1, 30 sec.; Line 2, 20 sec.; Line 3, 15 sec.; Line 4, 20 sec.

These four letters embody the exercise of first lesson. The same beginning oval may be used in making H and K if desired.

ATTACHED INSTRUCTIONS.

The same plan of "boiled down" instructions attached to the letters, as carried through Part III is also used here. Study them closely, as all are important points to be remembered and used in your practice.

Line 1. Note that the last part of the top of N is lower than the first, that the turn at the top is oval, and that the finish is a circle. Lay down a dime, draw around it and you'll have the idea. This finish may be a horizontal oval if desired, that is, the longest way horizontal.

Line 2. Begin **by the side** of the shade—**not in it.** Make letters narrow, down stroke almost a straight line on the main slant, and finish with stroke only two-thirds height of others.

Line 3. Keep letter narrow. Turns at top oval, and slanting downward, with circular finish like N.

Line 4. Try to connect the two parts of letter, but if you miss, cross as shown. Finish with circle as in M and N.

—85—

LESSON 3.

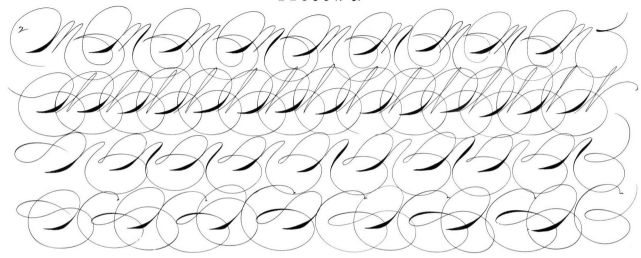

25 N's, 20 W's, 20 M's 20 X's a minute.

The pen is lifted once in the middle of each letter thus giving a chance to shift the paper and ink the pen.
Line 1. Besides the lift of pen in finishing the inverted oval, it is also lifted at the end of the letter, and begin there in making the next letter.
The other three letters are made with only one lift, the last part of the letter and the beginning of the next being **made with one continuous stroke.**

TOUCH.

Beginners in ornamental work usually have trouble with the pen. It has a tendency to stick in the paper, spatter ink, etc. Pressure on pen is too heavy. Ease up and touch paper lightly. Practice and care will overcome the difficulty. Even penmen sometimes have difficulty in getting the touch when changing to a finer pen. Don't always blame the pen for being scratchy, for it may be your heavy touch.

LESSON 4.

nnnnn nine noun ennui noun

mmmm mum minnie minim m

aaaaa anna manna ammonia

ccccc cannon commence cannon

ooooo onion common mammon

vvvvv venom move avenue vv

rrrrr runner mirror murmur r

sssss summons sessions missions

50 n's, 40 m's, 40 a's, 45 c's, 40 o's, 50 v's, 55 r's, 40 s's a minute.

Small letters are the same form as used in business writing, hence there is nothing new to learn except the light shades.

Every small letter except e, i, j and u should have at least one shade. A few letters, b, d, p, s and v, have two shades.

The shades on all letters in this lesson are light and should be made with a delicate, springy touch, so as to taper from a hair line to shade and from shade to hair line, without getting the shades heavy and abrupt. I recommend a trifle slower speed in making the shade on small letters, than used for the hair lines.

Read the attached instructions and make many lines of each copy.

—87—

LESSON 5.

Average from 6 to 8 words a minute.

Strokes must be quick enough to be smooth—free from all **kinks and wabbles.**

STICK TO YOUR COPY. Many persons do not make a success in life for the reason that they do not stick to one thing long enough to produce results. For the same reason many fail to learn penmanship. Stick to one thing till you can see some improvement. I don't, however, advocate spending days on one exercise without change. If a letter or exercise is especially hard, devote the most of your energy to it until a general improvement is noticeable. It is well, though, to change from one exercise to another, as in this way interest is the better maintained.

First study the letters of these copies carefully, then make page after page of each. Remember that no one can make a good letter without first knowing how it should be made, then giving it sufficient practice to train the nerves to execute the mental picture. As thinking makes the man, so thinking makes the penman.

LESSON 6.

Line 1, 50; Lines 2, 3 and 4, 40 a minute.

This principle is known as the **Capital Stem,** and three variations are given. The shade of the first two is the same as that of the inverted oval in preceding lessons, while in the last style the stem is completed by carrying the hair line around. Bring the shades well to the under part of the oval. Notice that the stem in the 1st, 3rd and 4th lines is **a compound** curve.

WORK. He who expects to excel in penmanship must realize that it requires work, both physical and mental. Practice, **alone,** won't acquire it; thought, **alone,** won't master it—the two must be properly combined if satisfactory results are to be realized.

HOW TO WORK. First, determine whether your movement produces perfectly strong, smooth and clean-cut hair lines and shades. If it doesn't your next job is to get it. Next is your touch uniformly light, delicate and artistic? If not get that. Next, do you know correct forms? If not, study until you do. Then the next and final task is that of acquiring such control of your hand as to enable you to put the pen reasonably near where you want it.

LESSON 7.

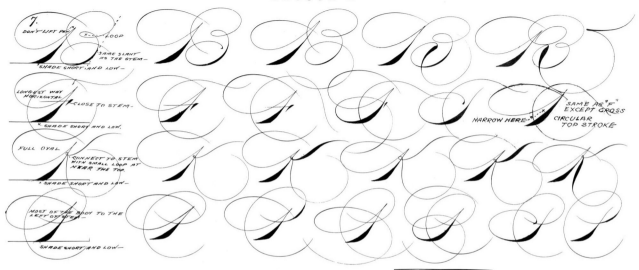

20 B's, 20 F's, 22 K's, 25 P's a minute.

These are letters embodying the **Capital Stem** principle which may be varied as shown by the different styles.

Read all the attached instructions—they are important.

The speed is indicated above for the purpose of giving the student a definite idea of the rapidity with which these letters should be made, therefore, it is hoped that it will be followed and that sufficient speed will be attained to insure strong, smooth hair lines, and bold, dashy shades. So long as kinks and wabbles are perceptible you may be sure the speed is insufficient.

It is not necessary to try to master the different styles of letters here shown, so select the styles preferred and make pages of them, always with a determined effort to improve from day to day.

LESSON 8.

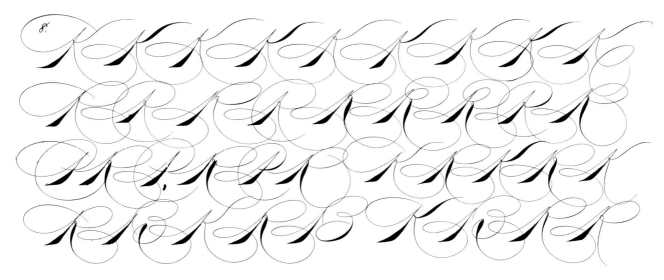

K's and R's 2½ to 3 lines (9 letters each), a minute.

The pen is lifted once on each letter, thus affording opportunity to shift the paper, and ink the pen. Keep the correct form in mind and do your best in this particular.

Unless you have made improvement by means of your practice on last lesson and are very well pleased with the results, it should be thoroughly reviewed before taking up another. By asking if you have mastered the work I don't mean to convey the idea that you should be able to make letters perfectly. We don't jump into great skill by cogs, by making one letter perfect before attempting another, but gradually,

LESSON 9.

i i i i i inning immure minnie

u u u u union unison unum

e e e e mennen mean meaning

w w w w winnow winner awning

j j j j juice major joyous jay

q q q q quart quince quenemo qu

jaw junior equine esquire quire

avenue sorrow mourner murmur

The 3 letter words, 20; 5 letter words, 15; 6 letter words, 12 a minute.

These are just the same forms as used in business writing and most of them are unshaded, however, other letters that should be shaded are given in the word copies. The other style of q may be used if desired.

If you have made up your mind to become a good penman, accomplish it. Don't be a "wishy-washy" sort of being who can't stick to a thing long enough for a reasonable person to have cause to expect success. A stubborn determination to succeed in an undertaking usually removes the barriers and makes success comparatively easy.

Compare your letters occasionally with the transparent Form Sheet in back of the book.

—92—

LESSON 10.

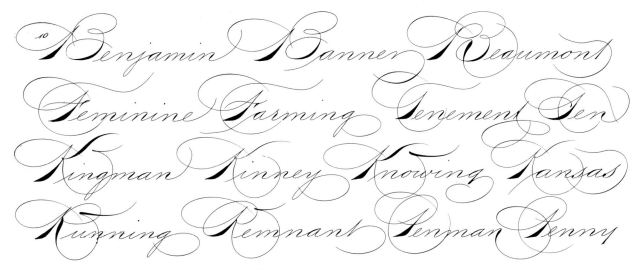

All about 7 to 8 words a minute.

    These words begin with capitals given in the two preceding lessons, the forms of which should be pretty well mastered by now.

    Begin with one word and write several lines of it, then another, and so on until all have been so written. The stroke ending the two K's in the 3rd line and the two R's in the 4th line is made by turning the pen around in the "Flourishing" position (see page 136) and the stroke thrown to the right.

    Are You Practicing regularly and faithfully, or spasmodically and impatiently? I find it a habit far too common among students to be in such a hurry to get to the end that they slight work. Too much skimming and changing from one thing to another. The best results come from thorough work as we proceed. Follow a plan of practice and do not leave a letter or exercise until **some** improvement can be seen.

LESSON 11.

C's 25 to 30, H's 22 to 25, S's 25 to 30, L's 25 to 30 a minute.

These are all rather difficult letters. Read and study the attached instructions.

Line 1. Note the shade of the first oval, get the turn at top of loop narrow, but not sharp, and taper the shades nicely so that the heaviest part of it is just above the crossing with the up stroke. Finish with a circle (like drawn around a dime) or a horizontal oval. It must be made quickly.

Line 2. The beginning oval and the last part is exactly the same as "C." Notice the long Compound curve connecting the two parts of the letter. Make quickly with a strong, sweeping motion with a slight increase in speed when the shade is begun.

Line 3. The beginning oval is same as for C. Note the **Compound** curve of the down stroke, that it crosses the up stroke at a point about half the height of the letter. The finish is the same as the **Capital Stem** in lesson 6.

Line 4. Exactly the same as "S" down as far as base line. A larger loop may be used at the bottom than here shown, if desired.

—94—

LESSON 12.

All about 12 groups a minute.

These groups are all made without lifting the pen and are, therefore, most excellent movement drills. Strive for uniformity in height, spacing and heaviness of shades. Make as many in a group as your movement will permit.

SCOPE OF MOVEMENT. The average good business writer has not sufficient scope to do good ornamental work. These exercises will assist in developing it, and in connection I recommend practice on movement drills given in Business Writing, Lessons 2, 5, 24 and Supplementary Exercises, pages 72 to 80. The muscles should be elastic enough to permit of making them 3 to 4 lines high. Do not use whole arm movement for any of these exercises.

LESSON 13.

UUUU tuning utter timid statement
ddddd deed indeed discard candid
attain sitting getting adding muddy
ppppp penman puny pompous pepper
ZZZZ zumans zeeman wizard zouave
xxxxx examine mixing maximum
expense extent expound constitution d
dexterity diamond penmanship added

t's 30, d's 30, p's 32, z's 40, x's 40 **a minute.**

"t's" AND "d's" AND HOW TO MAKE THEM SQUARE ON TOP. Few penmen, even professionals, have mastered the knack of squaring t's and d's with one stroke of the pen. Some even go as far as to assert that it can't be done. I have squared them with one stroke for years, and seldom, very seldom indeed, ever retouch one.

HOW IT IS DONE. Set the pen down at the **upper right-hand corner** of the letter, then bear on the pen with a rather heavy pressure, moving the **left** nib of the pen over to the left and keeping the **right** nib where it was first placed. After making the top in this way as broad as desired, gradually draw downward, relaxing the pressure until you finish at the base with a hair line; and, without lifting the pen, run upward with the finish.

By working from the above suggestion and making a careful study of every motion made, you can in a short time learn to make them. I would not convey the idea that it is easy to learn, for it is not, but any one who will practice thoughtfully and in an experimenting manner, can learn it.

—96—

LESSON 14.

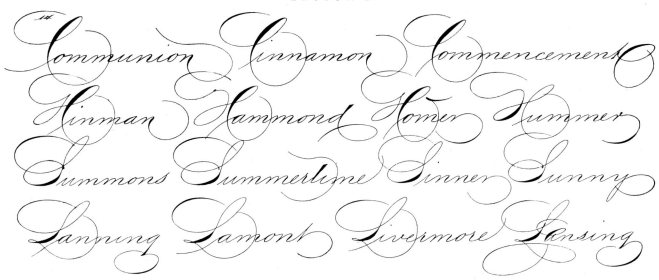

"Commencement" and "Summertime" about 5; "Hinman," "Homer," "Sinner," "Sunny," "Lamont" about 7 to 8; all others about 6 a minute.

Take these words one by one, practicing them separately, several lines of each. Begin the small letters close to the capital, watch the light delicate shades and get them as even and uniform as possible.

HARMONY is absolutely essential and is produced by intermingling shades with hair lines. Endeavor, so far as possible to avoid crossing shades. Hair lines should run parallel, else cross at right angles. They should never cross in **about** the same direction, nor be allowed to run into each other. It kills harmony.

Study spacing and arranging carefully, for herein lies much of the secret of its beauty.

Most capital letters have but one shade, and no letter is often given more than two shades. Occasionally a letter looks well with more than two shades, but they should be so placed that they harmonize and balance the letter. Hair lines should be fine and uniform in size.

LESSON 15.

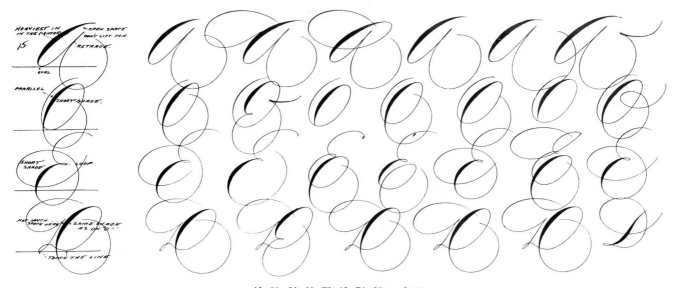

A's 30, O's 32, E's 32, D's 25 a minute.

These letters, like those of lesson 11, embody the direct oval. The shades are quite similar.

Line 1. In form the same as A in business writing. Finish with a circle, or horizontal oval if preferred. Different ways of beginning are shown.

Line 2. The shade of this letter is less slanting than that of "A." Get it to taper nicely. The first stroke may be shaded instead of the second if desired.

Line 3. Be careful about the slant of the letter, and note the connection loop. Several styles are shown.

Line 4. Begin with same oval as "C" and "H." Shade exactly same as "O." Circle or horizontal oval finish.

LESSON 16.

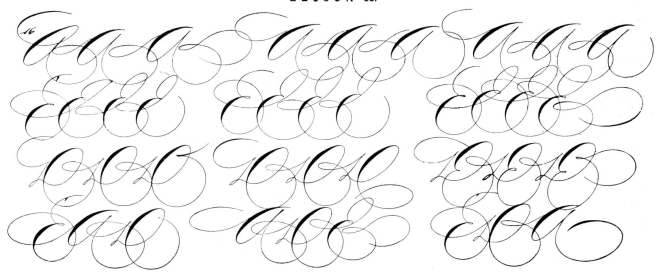

All about 10 to 12 groups a minute.

    The pen is not lifted for any of these, except in the first line. You should have sufficient movement to enable you to reach all points of these exercises.

    FORM. While speed, strength and dash of motion is urgently stressed, **form** must not be overlooked, nor its value underestimated. Freedom and snap of movement first; a uniformly light, artistic touch second; and accuracy of form third. Compare your letters occasionally with the transparent guide forms in the back of book, remembering that it is impossible to make correct letters until they are first so conceived in the mind. Be sure, then, you have a very definite conception of letters you are trying to make. You may then reasonably expect improvement.

LESSON 17.

lllll lilian million mullen miller

hhhhh hannah hummer hammering

bbbbb blaming blooming billing buy

kkkkk knack knock kimona making

fffff funny feminine furrow affair

ggggg gong going gunning gunner

yyyyy young yours synonym buying

hyhyhy hyena hymeneal hymnal high

l's 50 to 60; h's, b's, k's, g's and y's 40 to 50; f's 35 to 40 a minute.

The greatest difficulty in slant is usually encountered in making upper loops. To overcome the usual tendency to excessive slant in loops, make the first stroke WELL CURVED and standing fairly straight so that the down stroke, or back may be brought down in a straight line on the regular slant, without having to hump the back in order to get a loop. This is what occurs when the up stroke is not properly curved.

Try hard for uniformity of slant. Nothing so injures the appearance of writing as irregular, or uneven, slant.

A good way to overcome a fault is to practice the extreme for a while; hence if you have the fault of getting your loops or your writing in general too slanting, try making it too straight for a time. Practice on extremes often enable us to reach a desirable mean.

—100—

LESSON 18.

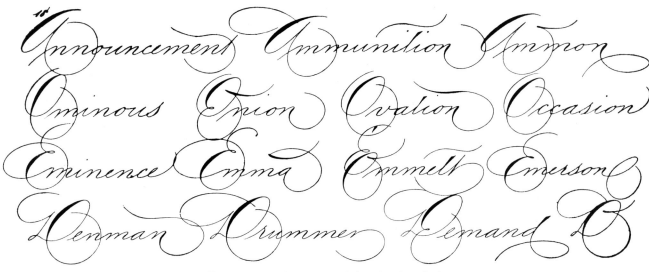

First two words about 5; rest of them 6 to 8 a minute.

    Practice these words separately, line after line of each, trying to get the speed indicated, yet maintaining accuracy.

    The contrast of shades and hair lines, combined with graceful curves and ovals, produce the striking beauty of artistic Writing. The smoother the shade and the finer and more delicate the hair line the prettier.

    Heavy, draggy lines never inspire, nor convince those who know, that the executor of them ranks very high as a penman.

    Life, vigor, and force must be put behind the pen, driving it with speed and boldness, sufficient to make smooth, clean-cut lines.

—101—

U, V and Y about 28 to 30; R about 25 a minute.

    These letters embody a new shade—a **Compound Curve** shade. After continued practice on the other shades this one will be found difficult. Remember, the bottom turn, after making the shade, must be oval. Note the various ways **to** beginning this oval, as shown in the different letters.

    If your capitals (shades or hair lines) should appear rough, kinky or wabbly, you may be reasonably sure the trouble is insufficient force and power—too slow speed. Increase the horsepower of your engine. It requires a lot of nerve force to produce strong, forceful penmanship.

LESSON 20.

Range from 5 to 12 words a minute.

Practice these words as usual, separately and line after line of each. Note the speed. Some may think my rate of speed too fast, but I wouldn't want one to write much slower. If this work is to be practical it must be done at a fair rate of speed. The amount of good work one can turn off in a given time determines, in a large measure, one's worth in any line.

Speed in writing is a growth up to a certain maximum degree. Not all can attain the same speed in writing any more than they can in running, or in executing certain kinds of work. We shall always have the slow, the fast, and all degrees between, but the extremely slow writers can increase speed with practice if they will, and still acquire accuracy. At any rate we must have smooth, clean-cut hair lines and shades and it requires speed and dash to produce them.

LESSON 21.

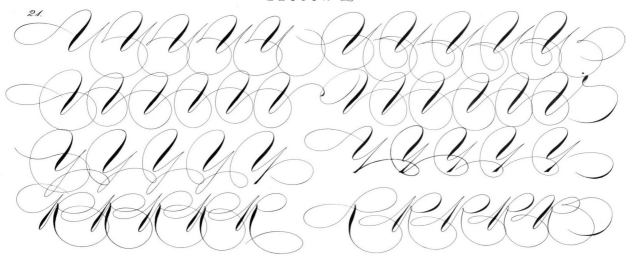

5 to 7 groups a minute.

IS IT YOUR PURPOSE TO BECOME A GOOD PENMAN? Then let nothing swerve you from that purpose. Determination is the power that makes the seeming impossible, possible; that digs through and scales mountains of difficulties. "Where there is a will there is a way." "Nothing is impossible to him who wills." "What man has done man can do." Let these be your mottoes. This quality of determination carries with it another quality, viz: ingenuity. If we are determined to do a thing we must often invent a new way. If we wish to drive a nail, and have no hammer, the determined, ingenious person takes a rock—just a different way to reach the same end. He who is determined to make a penman makes one, even if he hasn't an oblique holder, hand-made, with a handle a foot long. Some of the best penmen became such against great odds. Their chief instructor was a few poorly engraved copies, possibly from some college advertisement; their material the poorest, with possibly a wash stand for a table. But they got there. Lincoln didn't go to college, and had few books and fewer dollars, but he became an educated man. Johnson couldn't read when he married, but became President of the United States.

LESSON 22.

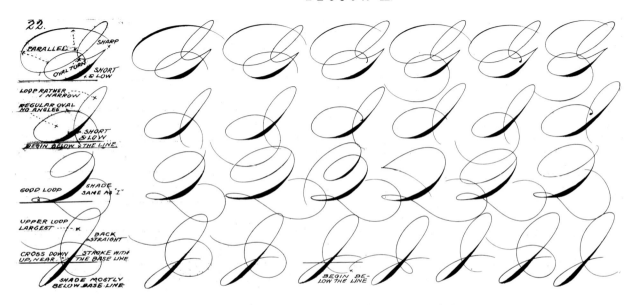

G's and Q's about 28; I's and J's about 35 a minute.

    Line 1. Begins same as S, and finish with inverted oval or capital stem shade. The point beginning the stem should be one-half the height of letter.
    Line 2. Begin **below** the line. Make the loop narrow and finish with the same shade as G.
    Line 3. The oval may begin any way desired. The shade is same as used on the inverted oval. Make loop same as on capital "L."
    Line 4. Begin **below** the line. The oval should be larger than that of "I." Make the back reasonably straight, with the shade about all below the base line.

LESSON 23.

5 to 6 groups a minute.

    More most splendid movement drills. Make as many connected as your movement will permit, or as the ink on the pen will allow. Note that the group of "l's" is made backward. Make these boldly, rapidly and as accurately as you can.

    Study the figures as closely as letters, for they are equally important. Remember that it is absolutely essential that we have a correct mental picture of a character in the mind before there can be any hope of being able to put it on paper. Then as you practice, **criticise.** Criticism is comparison of right with wrong. Study correct form, correct movement, correct habits of every nature and kind. When you see a few lines thrown together that fill your very being with enthusiasm, don't only glance and pass them by, but notice every detail, every curve, where lines cross each other, general proportion of height, spacing, etc., then with all this mental picture go to work determined to produce your ideal on your own paper, with your own pen and your own skill.

    Observe, work and criticise. Be a most severe critic of your work. Tear it all apart, and with thought, judgment and skill build it up again. Criticise! Criticise! if you would progress.

"We all guess more than we know."

LESSON 24.

"Germantown" and "Immunity" about 5; rest, 6 to 7 words a minute.

Practice line after line of each separate word as nearly at the rate of speed indicated as you can.

All can't write at the same speed, but if smooth, dashy lines are desired, good speed must be used. Snail-like motion will never get one anywhere in this business.

"Bear-up and steer right onward."

LESSON 25.

Speed: Z about 30; groups connected 6 to 8; "Zimmerman" 8; "Zealand" and "Zenith" 10 a minute.

Put lots of power and nerve force behind your pen in making these letters. Don't be discouraged if you don't get them well as quickly as you think you should.

Plod is the word. Patience and attention will win in the long run. If the cat sits long enough at the hole she will catch the mouse. It's up and down, up and down the field that plows the acres; there's no getting over the ground by a mile at a time. Great successes are of slow growth. Step by step, mile by mile, ends the journey, brick by brick houses are built; the last blow finishes the nail, and stroke by stroke the nerves are trained. Learn to labor and to wait. Brains grow by use as well as muscles. Nerves are trained by regular and faithful practice. Would you have fleeter feet? Try them in the race. Would you have stronger lungs? Use them in deeper and fuller breathing. Would you have a stronger mind? Put it at rational thinking, and if you would have steadier nerves use them with the pen.

"If you would be pungent, be brief."

LESSON 26.

    The common error in writing signature combinations is to scatter the capitals. They must be compact, close together, to look best. There is very little danger of getting them too close. Try to distribute the shades so the signature is well balanced. Don't place two or three shades close together, then leave a wide space with none. Cross lines as nearly at right angles as possible, avoiding nearly parallel crosses. In the signature "L. U. Crain" the hair line of oval between "L" and "U" crosses the beginning oval of "L" too nearly parallel. It would be better if the connecting oval were made a little larger, the bottom of it being brought lower. Get the shades of capitals of uniform heaviness.

"Manners are the ornament of action."

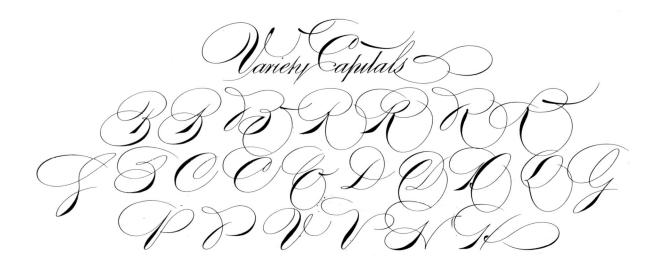

"Words are the voice of the heart."

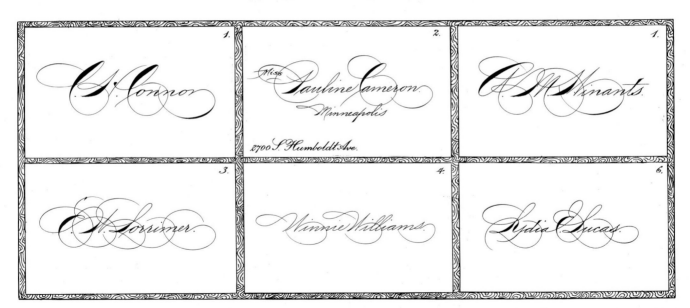

INSTRUCTIONS FOR PLATE ON PAGE 112, OPPOSITE.

This is the fascinating branch of penmanship art, and the goal desired to be reached by many aspiring penmen. Some make the mistake of undertaking it before a good artistic hand-writing is mastered. The order of learning should be, Business Writing first, then Artistic Writing which may be followed by Card Writing. Use a fine pen (Tamblyn's Professional No. 7) and an ink that produces a fine hair line.

Compactness: Equal distribution of shades; Intermingling of hair lines so as to balance; Delicacy of touch; Name just below the center of card and straight.

No. 1. "C. H. Connor" and "A. M. Winants." The shades are rather heavy, and the style same as previously given in lessons in Artistic Writing.

No. 2. The style is the same as No. 1, with lighter shade. The arrangement of address lines is one of a number of forms used. The prefix "Miss" may be written in same style as name, if desired.

Nos. 3 and 6. Same style as others with light shade similar to No. 2.

No. 4. Same style as others, without shade. Lines should be very fine and delicate; writing small and compact.

INSTRUCTIONS FOR PLATE ON PAGE 114, OVER.

IMPORTANT POINTS. Combined movement; considerable finger action, with enough Muscular to produce smooth, bold strokes. Name just below center of card and straight. Capitals uniform in height, also the small letters.

Practice on these cards should be preceded by study and practice on Engraver's Script, pages 115 to 119.

These styles are all but easy for the average amateur. Use a fine pen (Tamblyn's Professional No. 7).

No. 11. This unshaded style is popular, and easiest to execute. Get the name straight, with letters uniform in height. Make lines as fine as possible.

No. 12. These two styles are similar, although with different degrees of shade. The bottom one is a form of invitation to a party. The form may be varied to apply to any kind of party, luncheon, dinner, etc. The letters must be kept small and quite compact.

Nos. 13, 14 and 17. These are all heavy shaded styles.

No. 13 is a Business Card, No. 14 a personal visiting card showing that the lady is "At Home" to welcome callers on "Tuesdays." No. 17 is a Birthday Card, used principally by children and young people.

—113—

The cards may be ruled if difficulty is found in getting lines straight. A card may be folded near the middle, then cards to be ruled placed between the fold and with a sharp pencil make a very faint line along the edge of the folded card. The pencil line can be easily erased. The Tamblyn Card Ruler (price 10c) is excellent. The line made with this can be erased with a handkerchief or piece of cotton, so no trace of the line can be seen.

—114—

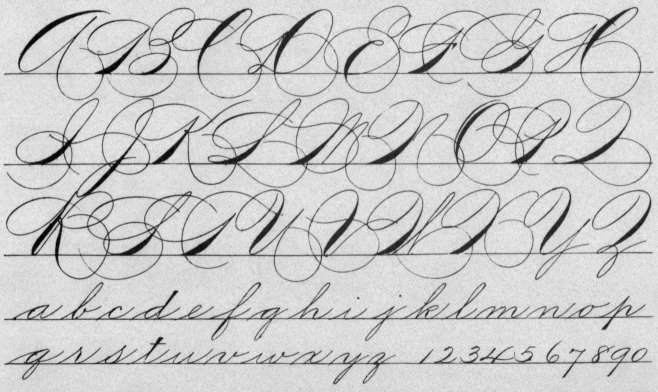

This is the style of penmanship not very popular with the amateurs yet indispensable and profitable to all who aspire to use their penmanship to greatest advantage.

The forms, as well as the movement required to make them, are so different from ordinary writing that it is rather discouraging. The forms must be memorized by study and practice as one would learn other things, while a somewhat slower motion must be employed. Use **Combined** movement, largely **Finger**, with enough muscular swing to make long lines smooth.

The capitals require more muscular movement than most of the small letters. Make all hair lines in capitals with a rapid, muscular movement swing, then slow down a little for the shade, using considerable finger motion on them.

Notice the attached instructions.

LESSON 1.

Same width all way down.

Cover end of hair line with the shade.

Make this short connecting line downward.

Lift pen here and cover the connection with the down stroke in "a" and the dot in "o".

summons runner murmur mirror

m's and w's about 20; the rest 25 to 30 a minute.

Note the attached instructions. Some lift the pen at the bottom of every down stroke with good results, but you will notice the pen is not lifted in making the round turns at bottom of u, i, n, m, a, o, c, etc.

It is really very important that the straight down strokes be of uniform width all the way down, as well as of uniform heaviness throughout the words. Work until you can get this. The hair lines are made faster than the shades. Refer to instructions for Lesson 13, Artistic Writing, page 96, for making shaded lines square at top and bottom.

"Judgment is the throne of prudence."

LESSON 2.

[Handwriting practice: letters j, y, g, q, z, z repeated; words: young quartz quizzing quenemo mug; juicy jaybird junior major quarrels; figures 1 2 3 4 5 6 7 8 9 0.]

Lift pen on the hairline

All letters about 20 a minute; "young" about 7; "quartz" 6; "quizzing," "quenemo" and "jaybird" about 5 a minute. The set of figures 25 to 30 seconds.

Instruction on last two pages apply here, also. Note that the pen is lifted in making the up-stroke of the j and g loop. This is done to avoid drawing the ink from the shade, which would result if the pen were run through the shade.

Dots and periods must be made carefully. Run the pen around until you get a round dot.

Figures require a great deal of practice.

"A good name is the best thing in the world."

—117—

LESSON 3.

same width all way down

Lift pen in making this shoulder.

/ / / / / *p p p p p p p* *f f f f f f*

l l l *b b b b b b* *h h h h h*

k k k k k *t t t t t* *d d d d d*

pink blinded tumbled hobble troubled

flank kink penman flattened millions

miscellaneous plenteous stupendous allies

p's, b's, k's and d's 18 to 20; l's and h's about 25; t's about 27 a minute.

These straight line down strokes are most difficult. It will require much practice to maintain a uniform pressure on the pen and draw down a perfectly straight line, free from kinks and wabbles.

Note the lifting of the pen on the up-stroke of the loops. The same applies to small "e." As you become more proficient you will probably make it without lifting the pen, but you will make a slight shoulder at the point marked **X** instead of making it one continuous curve, as in ordinary writing.

Square the tops and bottoms of letters by retouching where necessary, if you fail to get them square with the first stroke, as previously instructed.

—118—

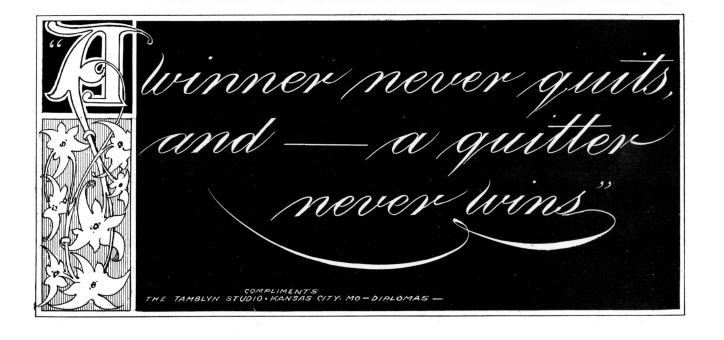

LETTERING & ENGROSSING

PLATE NO. 1.

Illustrating Pencil Outlining
AND BROAD PEN WORK BEFORE RETOUCHING ~

Marking Style   **Marking** Style

Old English   **German**

ROMAN ~ 123 &   GOTHIC

Lettering AND Engrossing — Tamblyn

    The light rough lines above indicate pencil lines. First draw the horizontal lines indicating height of letters, then the letters, lightly, merely indicating them. Beginners usually pencil too much. On the marking styles, and Old English, use a broad pen of the desired width, and make the strokes according to the numbers above and in the direction indicated by the **arrows**.

—120—

LESSON 1.

Medieval

ABCDEFGHIJKLMNOPQRSTU

12345 VWXYZ 67890

abcdefghijklmnopqrstuvwxyz abmvwy

This style of letter is made entirely with a broad pen without any retouching. Spacing is very important. All strokes must be made freely and easily.

Engrossers' Text

ABCDEFGHIJKLMNOPQR

12345 STUVWXYZ 67890

abcdefghijklmnopqrstuvwxyz fhtuvwyyz

The broad strokes are made first in this style, leaving room for the fine lines and retouching strokes which are then put on. Strive for a round white space inside letters.

LESSON 1. (Continued.)

12345 Marking 67890

ABCDEFGHIJKLM

NOPQRSTUVWXYZ

abcdefghijklmnopqrstuvwxyz &

F.W.Tamblyn – K.C.

Use a broad pointed lettering pen. Soennecken, or Gillott's of the desired width. A No. 2½ for letters about the size of copy. Hold the pen almost vertical and at such angle that the pen makes the hair lines on a slant of about 45 to 50 degrees. I can make finer hair lines and sharper points by filing the pen on the top side of point, making it thinner.

Use India Ink, Higgins or Bourgeois French (the latter preferred), slightly thinned with water. It is recommended that your practice be done crossways on ruled paper, using the ruling as guide lines to assist in getting the letters vertical. Rule top and bottom lines for height of letters. The sharp points on corners of shades are made by retouching with a fine pen.

LESSON 2.

Broad Pen Roman
ABCDEFGHIJKLMNOPQRSTUV
WXYZ

abcdefghijklmnopqrstuvwxyz 1234567890

Turn your pen further to the right for this style—make all basic or foundation strokes first. There is no retouching on the small letters and very little on the capitals, except the rounding of strokes around the center or white space of the letters and making a smooth joining of two strokes, as capital G—B—etc. These letters require more retouching than capital M—T—V—etc.

ABCDEFGHIJKLMNOPQRSTUVWXYZ&
abcdefghijklmnopqrstuvwxyz 1234567890

ABCDEFGHIJKLMNOPQRSTUVWXYZ
abcdefghijklmnopqrstuvwxyz-1234567890

Vertical and Slant Gothic. Both done with an ordinary rather blunt pen, else a speedball pen.

—123—

LESSON 2. (Continued.)

Modified Old English

ABCDEFGHIJKLM

abcdefghijklmnopqrstuvwxyz

NOPQRSTUVWXYZ

A rapid broad pen letter, very often used to replace straight Old English where time is important. It requires less time to execute as all strokes are made with a broad pen—fine lines are made by sliding the broad lettering pen sideways. If desired, fine lines can be put in the capitals with a ruler, which makes the style an imitation of straight Old English. It is very popular for filling diplomas, etc.

"Either never attempt, or accomplish."

—124—

LESSON 3.

BROAD PEN GOTHIC

A B C D E F G H I J K L M N O P Q R S T U
12345   V W X Y Z   67890
A B C D E F G H I J K L M N O P Q R S T U V W X Y Z

FINE PEN GOTHIC

A B C D E F G H I J K L M N O P Q R S T U V W X Y Z
a b c d e f g g h i j k l m n o p q r s t u v w x y y z

RAPID AND ARTISTIC   Plain and practical

The need for plain, rapid free-hand letters is always impressing itself upon a letterer who meets the requirements of the public. Here are styles that fill the bill. With absolutely no retouching required it becomes quite rapid, it is plain and artistic as well. They are well worth learning.

"Omit no opportunity to improve the mind."

LESSON 3. (Continued.)

Fine Pen Roman

A B C D E & F G H I J K L M N O P Q R S

1 2 3 4 5   T U V W X Y Z A   6 7 8 9 0

a a b c d e f g g h i j k l m n o p q r s t u v w x y z z

Because of its rapidily, with very little retouching,
this is a practical style of letter—one well worth learning.

These capitals are slightly retouched, but the small letters are not, hence it is a rapid style. Use an ordinary elastic writing pen in a oblique holder, although a straight holder can be used. Rule guide lines accurately and follow them with care. Bring every stroke exactly to the line, not short of it, nor through it. Imagine, if you can, the appearance of a printed page, wherein the letters are not uniform in height, and out of line, and you will see the desirability of getting your work accurate.

"An idle brain is the devil's workshop."

LESSON 4.

This is by all odds the most popular broad pen letter, and having so many appropriate uses, it should be thoroughly mastered. See illustration Plate No. 1, page 120, for the basic idea.

All broad strokes are made free-hand with the lettering pen. The curved hair lines are made with a fine pen, free-hand, and the straight hair lines with a ruler. Considerable retouching is necessary.

The dotted lines inside the letters "Old English" indicate where pencil marks should be made for outlining.

LESSON 5.

Free-hand Gothic

ABCDEFGHIJKLMNOPQRS
TUVWXYZ

abcdefghijklmnopqrstuvwxyz
This is done free-hand with a blunt or
worn writing pen, rapidly. without retouching

Draw guide lines for height of letters, and if necessary to outline the forms at first, stop it as quickly as possible. Learn to make it free-hand. A ball pointed pen, or one with a round point that will make about the same line in all directions, is best. Make every letter touch exactly the guide lines, so they will be uniform in height.

"Every man stamps his value upon himself."

LESSON 5. (Continued.)

GOTHIC

ABCDEFGHIJKLMNOPQ

RSTUVWXYZ.

abcdefghijklmnopqrstuvwxyz&

This is the standard Gothic alphabet. Draw top and bottom lines, and indicate position of letters with pencil lines. Use a ruler and broad pen for all heavy straight lines. Curved lines must be drawn free-hand, with a fine pen. This must be done carefully so that the lines will be of uniform width with the broad pen strokes, and the edges true and smooth. Draw outside lines of the curves with a fine pen and fill in between.

All retouching, points, fine lines, etc., are done with fine pen.

"The busy have no time for tears."

—129—

LESSON 5. (Continued.)

ROMAN

ABCDEFGHIJK

12345 LMNOP 67890

QRSTUVWXYZ &

This alphabet, as well as the Gothic, is familiar to every reader of English.

Use a ruler in making all straight lines. A broad pen for the heavy lines, and a fine pen for the light lines. The curved lines are done with a fine pen free-hand. In outlining the heavy curved lines, be careful not to get the lines too far apart, so as to make the shade too wide. It is easier to add width than to take it away, so get the outside lines too close rather than too far apart.

The small letters (lower case) are the same in both the Gothic and the Roman alphabets.

LESSON 6.

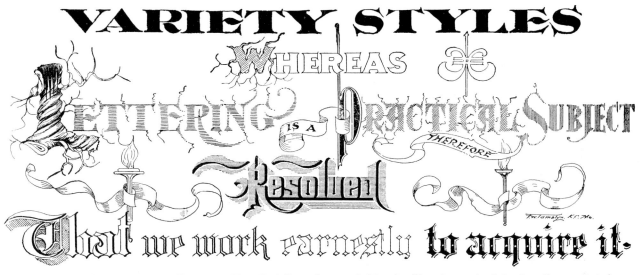

Most of this is done with a fine pen. The first line, the word "Resolved" and a part of the last line excepted.

"Resolved" was done on "Ross Board" which is a prepared board that comes ruled all over. There are various styles of ruling, so that numerous effects can be had by its use. This was ruled horizontally. The letters are outlined, the heavy black lines put on with a broad pen, and the surface of the board scraped away with a knife where the solid white appears.

The words "we work" are done with a double pointed pen.

"No legacy is so rich as honesty."

LESSON 6. (Continued.)

Edward G. Benjamin
No. 1. Old English–Plain.

Leonard Rand Parkington
No. 2. Modified Old English

Emily Dorothy Parnham
No. 3. Medieval Text.

Garrison C. Kinsman
No. 4. Flourished Script.

James H. Burnham
No. 5. Plain Script.

Styles

for

Lettering

or

"Filling in"

Diplomas

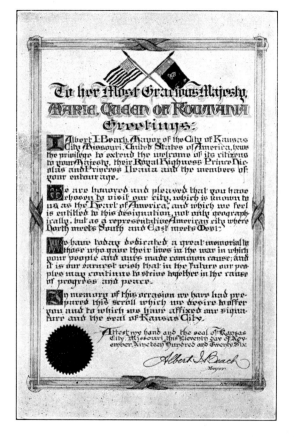
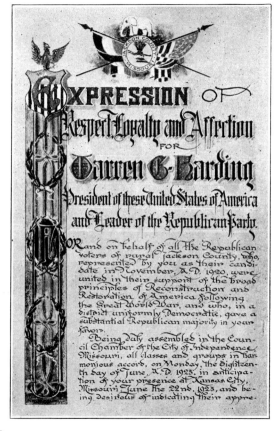

Illustrating the parts of birds, and the direction strokes are made. See position of holding pen on next page. Use Whole Arm movement for all large strokes. Many of the smaller ones can be made with muscular movement.

LESSON 1.

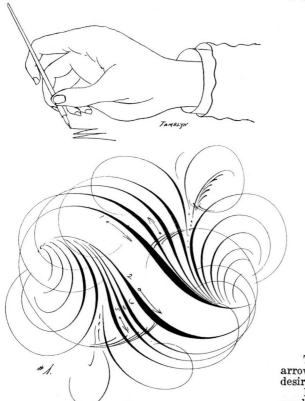

Illustrating position of hand and pen for flourishing.

Study this picture carefully and master the position before proceeding further. Sit at table the same as for writing.

Now start out on some of the strokes in the following. MAKE ALL HEAVY SHADES FROM THE BODY, instead of toward it, as we do in writing.

The small numbers indicate the strokes in order made, and the arrows the direction. The rest of them may be made in any order desired.
Make all strokes rapidly, with a strong, decisive motion. Each scroll should be made in about a minute.

LESSON 2.

    Don't imagine one can do this work well with finger movement, or even with a slow, creeping muscular movement. It must be done boldly, rapidly, freely. It is off-hand, free-hand work and can't be done right in any other way. This design should be made in from one and one-half to two minutes.

    Use a straight holder, with a flexible pen and follow the arrows, making the main strokes in the order indicated by numbers.

LESSON 3.

This is given to illustrate flourishing around a line of lettering. It is used quite appropriately on diplomas and certificate headings.

The flourishes should curve in harmony around the letters.

"Character is stronger than intellect."

LESSON 3. (Continued.)

Turn to page 135 for the direction of strokes. The order in which they should be made is indicated by numbers above. Strive for freedom of motion, so as to make strong, smooth lines. There must be only one stroke of the pen for each line, no retouching. This complete design should be made in about one to one and one-half minutes.

"False friends are worse than open enemies."

The direction of strokes is indicated by the arrows, and the order of them by the numbers. The complete design should be done within two minutes.

"The wretched have no friends."

LESSON 5.

Each line is made with a single stroke of the pen without any retouching. The cross-hatching at end of the scroll is done with the pen in flourishing position. The design should be done in a minute.

"The wasteful man shall live to want."

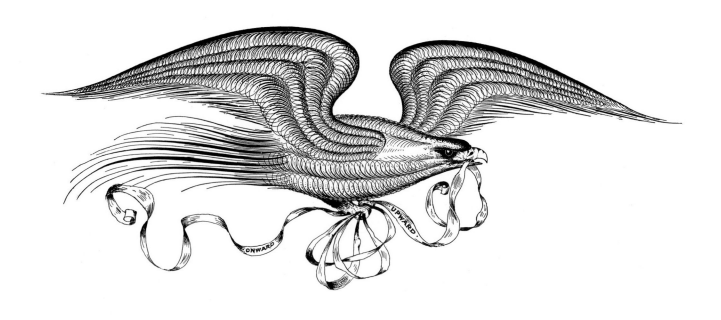

POPULAR MECHANICS ADVERTISING SECTION

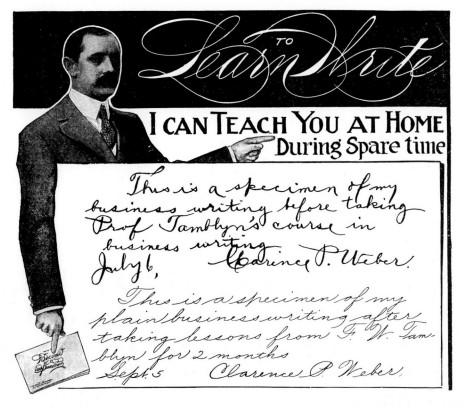

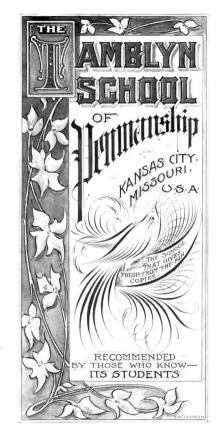

Artistic Engrossing and Illuminating

of

Resolutions, Testimonials, Memorials, Diplomas, Addresses, Shingles, Charters, Honor Rolls, &c.

on Cardboard, Parchment or Vellum

F.W. TAMBLYN STUDIO

of Designing, Engrossing and Illuminating

RIDGE BLDG., KANSAS CITY, MISSOURI.

PHONE VICTOR 5239.

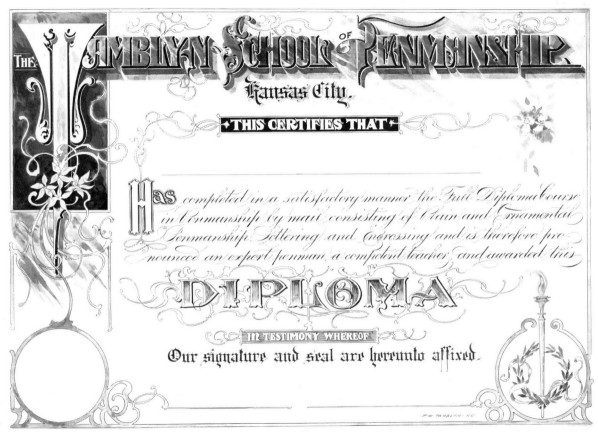

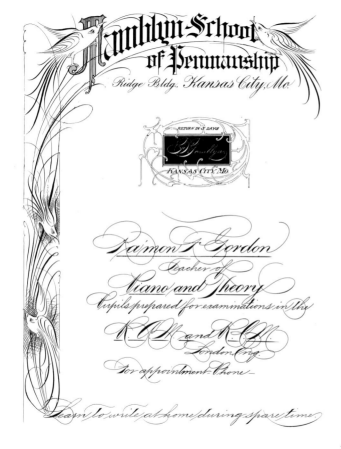

RESOLUTION

Adopted by the Board of Directors of

Central Surety and Insurance Corporation

at its meeting of February 13, 1934.

We are inexpressibly saddened by the death of our friend, Chairman and Director,

Peter W. Goebel

From the inception of this Company he was with us, a pillar of strength and support. His friendly counsel, clear vision and fine judgment were at all times at our command. In the realm of citizenship and philanthropy he gave the utmost of himself and means toward the relief of the needy and underprivileged of Kansas City. His personality and nobility of character coupled with the simplicity of his life, endeared him to all who had the privilege of knowing him. He was especially active in his church affairs, and was in every sense of the word, a Christian gentleman. A truly distinguished civic leader and beloved associate has passed on, leaving a great void, but leaving to us a memory of deeds and idealism which we will always cherish.

Resolved, that the foregoing resolution be entered upon the records of Central Surety and Insurance Corporation, and that an engrossed copy thereof be sent to the widow and children of our beloved friend and associate.

President.

Secretary.

Chairman of Resolution Committee.

RIDGE BUILDING · KANSAS CITY · MO · USA

DIPLOMAS

Penmanship, Public School Drawing
and Comic Cartooning Taught by Mail.
Diplomas,
Resolutions, Memorials, Calling Cards,
and all kinds of fancy pen-work
executed To order. Prices reasonable.
C. M. Wright.
PENMAN
E. T. College.
Commerce, Tex.

H. K. Burch.

T. J. Mathey.

H. Thompson.

W. G. Yocum,

N. Chitwood.

John W. Newlin.

Make Opportunities

Lost Opportunities

Riverside Business College

Independence Business College

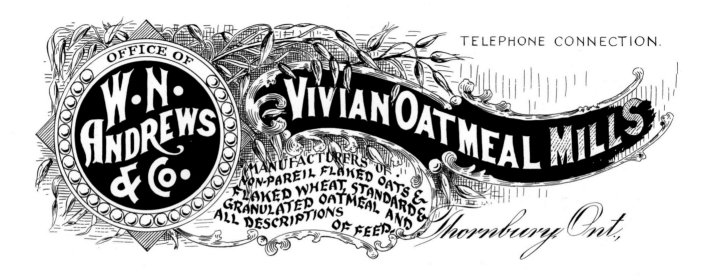

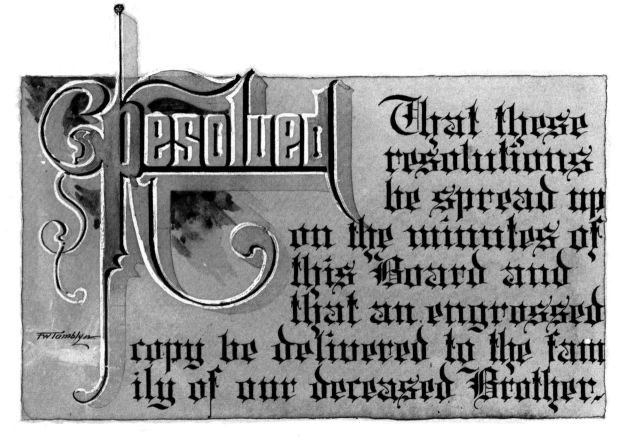

RESOLUTIONS
ADOPTED BY
The Commercial Club of Kansas City, Missouri,
DECEMBER 5, 1905. ON THE DEATH OF
AUGUST ROBERT MEYER.

Death has once more invaded this club, and taken from us a man of rare usefulness and a most valued member. On December first, August R. Meyer, a former President of this organization, passed to the Great Beyond. Truly, in this instance, Death sought a shining mark. Our friend has gone beyond the limits of our present vision, but he has left enshrined in our hearts a fragrant memory, and behind him is a record of well doing, that should be an inspiration to us all. He made a brave struggle; there was much for him to live for, but his mortal part could resist no longer, and, in his prime he has fallen. It is hard, indeed, to realize that the active personality, that so impressed itself upon all who met him, is no longer here, and that the noble heart is stilled.

August R. Meyer was nature's nobleman; not self made. God made. Those supreme qualities of head and heart, which in their after fruitage ripened into so princely a manhood, were his endowment at birth. Accidents of fortune and environment might have changed or modified the activities in which his life found expression; but the rare quality of his generous and noble impulse would have graced and glorified any calling or station. In the splendid composite of his nature, selfishness and greed never found a place, and his greatest happiness came from his efforts for the help and betterment of others.

To this noble birthright, Mr. Meyer was ever true. As we look back upon his life, now so suddenly closed here, how noble and how beautiful it was. Never marred by an ignoble thought or deed, it stands forth radiant with goodness, with benefactions, with charity and beautiful living. His was a success never acquired at the expense of others, and none of the many victories in his life ever involved another's downfall.

His high ambition was ever to beautify and better the condition of his neighbor, his state, and his country. Kansas City is fortunate to have had in her midst, for so many years, so splendid a citizen and man, and the legacy of his life is a priceless municipal heritage. For generations to come our people will hold him in loving memory, and fathers will point their children with pride to the life and deeds of A. R. Meyer, and bid them emulate his example.

It can not be that this life, into which was blended so much of beauty, of kindness, of nobleness, and strength, has ended with the accident of death. It must be that God, in His wisdom has found a higher sphere of activity for the trained and ripened faculties and powers of our friend, in the immortal life which He has bid him enter and in which he will live and grow.

Be It Resolved

That, in the death of August R. Meyer, The Commercial Club of Kansas City has lost a most valuable member, and the City a steadfast friend.

Resolved

That, this Club extends its heartfelt sympathy to the family of our late companion, who are now in the shadow of this great sorrow. May the tender memories of the many virtues of husband and father tend to lighten their burden and soften their grief.

Resolved

That a copy of this preamble and the resolutions be spread upon the minutes of the Club, as evidence of the high esteem in which our departed friend was held in the estimation of the business interests of the city; and

Further Be It Resolved

That a copy of the resolutions be sent to the family of A. R. Meyer.

Attest:

_____

SECRETARY.

_____ CHAIRMAN.

_____

_____

F. W. TAMBLYN. PENMAN—

At a meeting of the Board of Directors of the
Kansas City Live Stock Exchange

HELD   MARCH 31, 1903

The following was unanimously adopted:

WHEREAS, The members of the Kansas City Live Stock Exchange are again most sadly and forcibly reminded of the frailty of human life by the sudden removal from their number of

GUSTAVUS F. SWIFT.

Viewed from any standpoint he was a most admirable and a most colossal character. His concepts in temporal affairs were as broad as the world and were realized and effectuated by a matchless organizing and executive ability, coupled with an indomitable energy, which brushed aside obstacles before which ordinary hearts would have quailed. Like some tall oak of the forest, which because of its gigantic proportions encountered the severest blasts; yet stood while weak-

RESOLUTIONS

On the death of Mr. R. M. Scruggs.

In the death of their friend and eminent fellow-citizen

Mr. Richard M. Scruggs,

the Directors of the Bethesda have lost a true friend

For his honorable and useful life they are grateful; to his true and unwavering friendship, his systematic and unostentatious benevolence, his spotless integrity, his largeness of heart, they bear witness. His tender sympathy for human needs they know.

With all the pleasant memories that will cluster evermore about his name, in recognition of his magnificent gifts to the Incurables, their Hospital, to the Old Ladies Home, their lot, and for his last legacy, $25000.00, they add their testimony to his beneficence, and subscribe thereto upon the records.

In loving acknowledgment of his services to their association, they join the various other Charities and Institutions with which he was connected, the circle of friends nearest and dearest to him, and the Citizens of St. Louis by whom he was so severely esteemed, in this memorial, and they present this testimonial to the public at large and direct that a copy be forwarded, with the expression of their tender sympathy, to the sorrowing members of his family.

"He rests from his labors and his works do follow him."

Roger Hayne, Secretary
E. W. Saunders, M.D., President

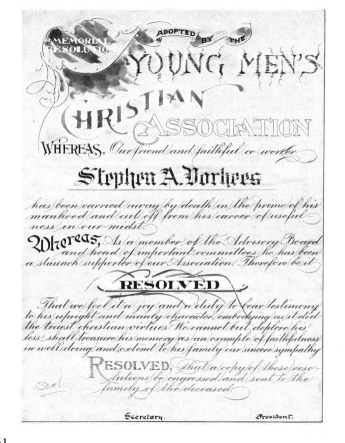

MEMORIAL RESOLUTION ADOPTED BY THE YOUNG MEN'S CHRISTIAN ASSOCIATION

WHEREAS, Our friend and faithful co-worker

Stephen A. Vorhees

has been carried away by death in the prime of his manhood and cut off from his career of usefulness in our midst.

Whereas, As a member of the Advisory Board and head of important committees he has been a staunch supporter of our Association. Therefore be it

RESOLVED

That we feel it a joy and a duty to bear testimony to his upright and manly character, embodying as it did the truest christian virtues. We cannot but deplore his loss, shall treasure his memory as an example of faithfulness in well-doing, and extend to his family our sincere sympathy.

RESOLVED, That a copy of these resolutions be engrossed and sent to the family of the deceased.

Seal

Secretary.   President.

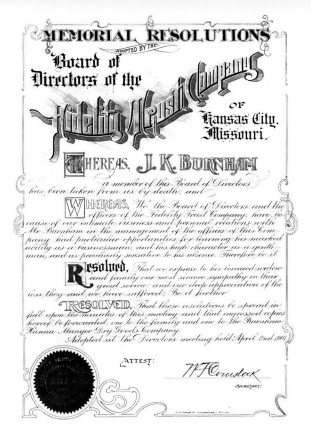

IN MEMORIAM
James B. Jackson

Whereas in the passing of James B. Jackson, the School System of Kansas City, Missouri, has lost a warm and valued friend his place will be hard to fill. In his many years of service he had accumulated a wealth of knowledge that was written; much of this he has taken with him to fill the hours till his loved ones come.

In the removal of this link from lifes chain, we are again reminded that as the chain is shortened from time to time, the Holder is gradually drawing us nearer and nearer to the haven of eternity. For our own sakes we selfishly grieve for the one who has left us we must believe that in some way not understandable to finite minds, it were better so leading us to repeat the comforting words of an abiding faith, "Thy will, not ours, be done". Therefore, be it

Resolved, That to the loved ones left we offer the consolation of faith and hope, secure in the belief that these will help to bridge the gaps of loneliness and heartaches Be it further

Resolved, That a copy of these resolutions be spread upon our minutes, and a copy be engrossed and sent to Mrs. Jackson

President K.C.Mo.School Board

Attest:

Acting Secretary

Editorial, The Kansas City Star
April 6th, 1926.
E.M.Clendening, Guest of Honor.

The master of occasions and ceremonies becomes the guest of honor. Distinguished service is given affectionate recognition. In paying tribute to Mr. E. M. Clendening tonight the Chamber of Commerce makes a tender of esteem and love to one who has represented it in varied capacities, has largely directed its affairs and still occupies a post of recognized importance in its activities and counsels.

Thirty-three years ago Mr. Clendening was made secretary of the Commercial Club. Nine years ago he was appointed assistant to the president of the Chamber of Commerce, the renamed organization. In these years this highly efficient, affable and popular officer has had an extraordinary contact. First with the commercial establishments and their personnel in this city. Then with the ranging roster of regional and national business organizations. Finally with men of the first rank in national affairs and public office. He has represented his organization in conventions and as scout extraordinary. He has come in touch with most of the Presidents of the United States, many cabinet members and governors in this more than three-score period. He has become an authority on what may be called procedure in the big things business organizations undertake.

When such service is supplemented by the even temper, the intelligent consideration, the sense of humor and ingratiating manner that always have been characteristics of Mr. Clendening's, affection attends appreciation

The hanging of a portrait of Mr. Clendening where the portraits of only two other officials of the Chamber of Commerce have been hung, is a particularly fitting tribute to one still active in the service thus recognized It will be a jolly occasion with lots of heart in it.

Ritz-Carlton Academy of Dancing

HAVANA · NEW YORK · LONDON

To all whom it may Concern:
THIS IS TO CERTIFY THAT

Has taken a complete course of instruction in modern dances and upon examination by the Board of Directors of this Academy, is worthy the Title of

Professor of Modern Dances

specializing the Tango, Maxixe, Danzon, and One Step. This Academy, therefore, affixes its official seal and signatures corresponding.

Given at Havana, Cuba, this _____

_____   _____
Secretary   President

_____
Instructor

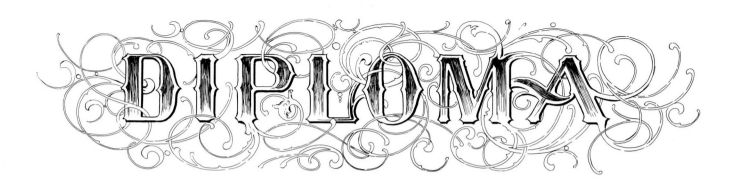

DIPLOMA

FOR having completed in a satisfactory manner the correspondence course in _____ as prescribed by _____

Given under our hand and seal this _____ day of _____ Nineteen hundred and _____

THE WICHITA
COLLEGE OF MUSIC

ESTABLISHED 1906. INCORPORATED 1907.

To all to Whom these Presents shall come, Greeting:

The State Industrial Department
at Western University

QUINDARO KANSAS

NORMAL COURSE

This Certifies That

School of Commercial Science
Greenville College

Given at Lee's Summit, Missouri this ninth day of May in the year of Our Lord one thousand nine hundred and one

More home Pupils and successful students than any Business College South.

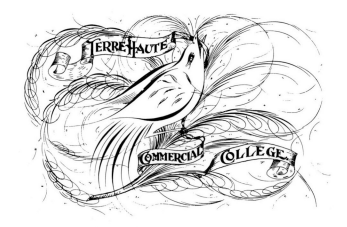